Points North and West

Points North and West

Janet Barclay

Loose Cannon Press

LIBRARY AND ARCHIVES CANADA CATALOGUING IN PUBLICATION

Barclay, Janet, 1947-, author
Points north and west / Janet Barclay

Includes bibliographical references
ISBN 978-0-9936881-3-3 (pbk.)

1. Barclay, Janet, 1947- --Travel. 2. Canada, Northern--Description and travel. 3. Alaska--Description and travel. 4. Northwest Territories--Description and travel. I. Title

FC38.B37 2014 917.104'73 C2014-902814-8

Published by
LOOSE CANNON PRESS

loosecannonpress@gmail.com
www.loosecannonpress.com

Table of Contents

Acknowledgements

I would like to thank my husband Bob for all his support and encouragement in making this book a reality. Big thanks go to Gwen Zilm who did all the driving so we could do the wine tasting in the Okanagan; to Mike and Kathy Gates, our friends and tour guides in Whitehorse; and for the ongoing support from our friends at Ottawa Camping Trailers. I am also grateful for all the feedback from friends and family members, without whose support this book would not have happened.

Chapter One
Introduction

We became involved with camping when our three oldest children were young—aged between six and ten—and became avid car campers, relying very heavily on tents and air mattresses. I like to emphasis the heavily, because our first tent was one of those solid canvas ones that weighed down the back of whatever vehicle we were driving, and took at least two people struggling with the weight to erect it. Gradually we moved to much lighter tents, and more of them, as the family grew to include our fourth child, but were always very dependent on our dining tents which provided us with shelter on those wet and windy days. Throughout this time we poured scorn on all those camping with trailers or RVs; that wasn't *real* camping!

Tenting on Grand Manan Island with our VW Vanagon and canvas tents

The first few years took us to many places across Canada; right across to Vancouver for Expo '86; down East to Grand Manan Island in New Brunswick; to Georgian Bay (when it was too cold and damp to camp in Algonquin Park); and to so many points in between. But we never made it up North. That remained a dream, and one of those places we really wanted to go sometime in the future.

Over those 25 years we camped with our small children and watched them grow up to enjoy the camping experience themselves, and in their turn to pass this enjoyment on to their children; including the swimming, the campfires, burnt marshmallows and wieners, the wildlife, and hearing the wolves in Algonquin Park, to mention but a few. By then the air mattresses had given way to cots for the now older generation—the knees and backs just wouldn't take lying on the ground—but the joy of camping still remained. Then came our epiphany.

Once we had retired, we promised ourselves we would follow the Tour de France. We had been fans of that great race for many years and thought it would be wonderful to see it in person. We had no real idea of what to expect, but realized that we would need some sort of vehicle to do this, and if we were going into the mountains to follow the riders, then that vehicle would have to be an RV or, as they are called in France, a camping car.

The experience was wonderful; we saw small, out-of-the-way places in France that we normally would never have seen, and learned the luxury of being a snail and taking your home with you.

Back in Canada we returned to camping in tents once more, but for some reason it had lost its appeal! We're not sure why. Perhaps having to get up in the middle of the night to wander through the campground looking for the washroom had something to do with it? Perhaps it was the rough ground we slept on? Who knows? We talked about buying or renting an RV, but no... well, maybe... well... let's see.

The view from above; our camping car (centre left) among others at the Tour de France

Then came the final tent camping trip! We went camping with our son, his wife and two very small girls, and the weather began glorious; a typical summer day. We had forgotten the other side of those days. By the late afternoon the humidity had increased, the skies had clouded over, and the heavens opened. We had brought the dining tent, which meant we could keep fairly dry, and there was space for the two little girls to play. However, after about 30 minutes, the campsite was flooded, and everything was damp. Oh well! That's camping. We dried the sleeping bags out in the campsite laundry room, cleaned up the mess, and generally made everything unpleasant go away. The next day dawned warm and sunny, but by mid-afternoon the sky once more clouded over, and this time the clouds were blacker than ever. Once again the heavens opened, and once again the campsite was flooded, and once again the sleeping bags were wet, and once again we went to the laundry room... and there everything changed. The storm had taken out the Hydro and the laundry room and all the facilities we depended on were without power. Even the standpipes were running incredibly slowly because there was no electricity to power the pumps! As always we coped, but while some of that camping trip was fun, there were things we were just not happy about.

Now we really cast our minds back to that trip in France and all the fun and security of having an RV. We were converts in the making.

So started the search for the perfect vehicle. We didn't want a trailer because that would mean buying a more powerful car; our little Toyota Echo just wouldn't do. So eventually we decided on a small RV. We visited many dealerships in the area with little success, but we did learn what we *didn't* want. What we *did* want was a bed that didn't have to be folded up, shower and toilet in separate enclosures, and reasonable space for cooking and dining. We checked websites for both new and used vehicles and kept telling ourselves that we would buy a vehicle the following year. We should have known better than to say that.

During our research we found Ottawa Camping Trailers, a friendly dealership in South Ottawa. We told the salesman Pierre what it was we were looking for—"But, of course, we are looking to buy next year, Pierre"—and, of course, he had the perfect RV for us right there on the lot! We fell in love with it, and after deliberating for all of 24 hours we returned and bought it. And we haven't looked back...

Posing beside our brand new RV

Now we had the means to travel, we had to think about where we wanted to go. Florida beckoned and we responded; then we went to antique car rallies towing our 1929 Morgan three-wheeler on its trailer; and we camped with the grandkids, a great idea as they slept above the cab and loved it. The more we used it, the more we loved our RV, and so we planned more and more adventures. Now, finally, we could take that dream trip and travel up North. Initially we were going to do this in the summer of 2011, but due to family commitments we had to put it off until 2012. This was a good thing because we gained more experience in RVing and made a number of changes to the vehicle, all of which made it more comfortable for us.

At an antique car rally in Stowe, Vermont with our 1929 Morgan Aero (the green one)

The journey described in this book would last about eight weeks, ending at a family wedding in Ontario at the end of August. Other than that we were footloose and fancy-free, with the ambition to drive up the Dempster Highway to Inuvik and to see some of Alaska on the way home. So the planning began.

We finally left Ottawa on June 29, 2012 for *Points North and West.* This is the story of our adventure.

Chapter Two
Planning

Planning for this trip was in two parts: firstly, we would be traveling and living in our RV for a much longer period than we had so far, so we had to get our heads around that idea; and secondly we needed to plan where exactly we would go, how long it would take to get there, what we wanted to see, and... and... and... When we really thought about it we flinched, looked rapidly away, and then tried to focus on the overall trip, not getting too bogged down in the specifics. After all, on previous trips we had more or less let the schedule develop as it would day by day, having only large, overall destinations more or less established.

Planning for a trip of about two months was quite something. The longest we had been out in our own RV was two weeks, and we had managed that quite well. Our trip to France had been nearly four weeks in the rental RV, but that felt different because we were away from home and having our first experience of RV traveling. So, part of the planning meant that every time we went out for even a few days, we thought about what else needed to be done to the vehicle, or what other equipment we might need to make life more comfortable over a longer period. We would come back home with a list of things to do, change, make and buy. Fortunately, we didn't need to do it all at once.

On one never-to-be-forgotten trip I drove down to southern Indiana to meet Bob, a two- to three-day drive, mainly on highways and so not too bad... until I met the highways of Michigan! At that point it seemed that every road I drove on was either under repair or should have been. I drove with a cacophony coming from the back; at times the cutlery was literally being shaken out of the drawers and the cupboards were bursting open. These roads were terrible and I heard the result while driving. In those rather fraught moments I realized that proper padding for everything that could rattle was going to be essential for our proposed trip to Inuvik. In all fairness to the RV, most of the time, and on reasonable but not necessarily good roads, there were no worries about the extra noise of things going astray in cupboards. This only happened in extreme conditions, like the surfaces of Michigan highways!

So, over the winter I made lots of padded bags to fit the variety of pots and pans we used. The cutlery also needed padding, so before the trip I made nice old fashioned rolls with individual pockets for each item, so the noise factor would be reduced. Bob also adapted the drawer for tableware so the plates and bowls all slid firmly between dowels or sat in recesses so they didn't shift around. Sometimes trying to get plates out of the slots became annoying because they fitted so well!

I thought a mat near the sink would be a nice touch in the RV, so when I saw a passenger on a ferry in North Carolina making one, I asked her about it. As a result I bought the supplies at the store in Manteo she had recommended, and subsequently made my own pretty rug. One more thing off the to-do list.

An important installation was a wine rack. Our experiences during the Tour de France convinced us that the end of any day of driving was best celebrated with a good bottle of local wine. It was simple to build a rack from wood and insert it into one of the upper cupboards.

Kitchen mat and storage unit for boots and shoes

In our tent-camping days shoes of every description were always left outside the tent or in the car, but as we soon found out, that didn't work in the RV. They always had to come inside with us, so shoe storage became a problem for Bob to solve. Construction of a shallow bin just beside the door ensured that shoes were where they needed to be, and we didn't trip over them.

Now, a brief word about our meals. We have long been proponents of proper meals when we are camping, and even when tent camping I would cook chicken, pork chops, spaghetti, etc. Not for us the traditional hotdogs and hamburgers (other than hotdogs over the campfire) so traveling in the RV was no different. We had a stovetop and microwave in the RV but no oven, which on a long trip would be an issue, so the answer was the Infrachef. Friends of ours in West Virginia had one and I remembered seeing how useful it was. As I was wondering where to find one, I learned that our favourite camping store, Ottawa Camping Trailers, had them on sale. After chatting to some of the staff members, and receiving rave reviews, we bought one. I cooked a very moist roast chicken and a couple of batches of muffins at home and I happily added this device to the RV. Now I really could cook!

The Infrachef and the newly installed cupboard

As usual with such a small living area, everything needed to have its own place, including those annoying boxes of plastic wraps and storage bags. Soon Bob was on that project. He added a small cupboard to the interior of the vehicle, designed with our needs in mind. A door and attachment hardware were ordered from Coachman to match all the other fittings in the RV and, bingo, those messy boxes and rolls were safely and tidily stored away, ready for use when needed.

We bought collapsible bins for use in the storage areas of the vehicle, and these allowed us to organize the extra things needed for this trip. Then it was time to look at our bikes. It wasn't practical to attach bikes to a rack on the back of the vehicle, given the drive we were planning, so we bought collapsible bikes—they really are compact when folded—and a space was found for them in the main storage area, ready for use when needed.

One of Bob's dreams for this trip was to spend his birthday under the midnight sun. We knew that as we traveled north the nights would become shorter and shorter, so as an aid to sleep I made blackout (or should I say brownout) curtains to cut the light down and allow us to maintain reasonable sleeping patterns.

We had heard stories about the Dempster Highway and how tough it was on tires, and it was clear that more tools would be needed. We already had the usual toolkit of screwdrivers, pliers, hammer, etc (no RV is complete without those) but we added a large torque wrench for the wheel nuts, a substantial hydraulic jack, two plastic gasoline cans, and a spare tire on a rim.

Things were definitely getting organized.

Gradually our list was getting shorter and we were feeling that this trip was really possible. The last major thing we had to work out was clothes. Not the everyday traveling clothes, but those suitable for a wedding. At the end of the trip we would be in Walkerton, Ontario for a family wedding, so 'wedding clothes' had to be packed as well! They were put in a separate suitcase and placed at the back of the large rear storage area. Once that little dilemma was sorted out, we felt ready to go. In fact, one might say, anxious to go.

How far we could reasonably travel per day was the next issue to be tackled. We have both driven a variety of vehicles over the last several decades, and have come to the conclusion that our tolerance for driving for an extended period is about six hours, no matter what the vehicle. We had followed this routine in 1986 when we crossed Canada with our three children to visit Expo '86 in Vancouver. We all tolerated it well, so this became our driving pattern for most of our subsequent journeys. Along with that we needed to sort out the division of labour. Since I tend to fall asleep after lunch—which isn't a very good idea when driving—I would take the morning shift and Bob would drive after lunch. This had worked well for us on previous trips, so why break a winning pattern? By driving for about six hours a day we could cover about 500-600km, although we always kept the schedule flexible enough to either stop a little earlier or drive a little longer, depending mostly on campsite availability. On extended trips we would also include short driving days to allow for time to catch up with chores. Even on vacation there are always things that need to be done.

Having dealt with all the practicalities of extended travel, it was time to decide exactly where we were going, and to learn as much as we could about all the places we wanted to see. We spoke to friends who had driven up North; talked to a neighbour who had lived in Inuvik for a while; and learned more about the town and the Dempster Highway. We sent off for tourist information for the Yukon, Northwest Territories, British Columbia and Alaska; read Hazel Johnson's *RV-ing and Other Adventures North of 60;* and bought *The Milepost.* This book is a must-have for anyone contemplating this kind of travel. It takes you through the north west of Canada and Alaska in incredible detail. Every major road is described kilometre by kilometre (and in miles too) and the road maps give the readers/travelers a good idea of where they are actually going. It describes restaurants, look-offs, campgrounds, gas stations, scenery, wildlife, history. You name it, it's in there. *The Milepost* became our Bible on the road, and its well thumbed pages attest to that.

Our final plans had to be rather loose because we didn't know exactly what we would encounter. However, there were two fixed dates: we had booked a ferry from Haines, Alaska to Prince Rupert, British Columbia before we left, and we had to be back for that wedding in Walkerton, Ontario with enough time to make ourselves reasonably presentable.

We also hoped to see friends in Whitehorse, Yukon, so we allowed for a couple of days there, and on the way home we wanted to spend time with a friend in Kelowna and do some wine tourism in the Okanagan Valley. Anything else we did would be a bonus. So within these parameters established we started to plan the rest of our trip.

The first and most important place we felt we must visit was Inuvik. My mother had been there many years before with an organization called Elder Hostel and we were envious and wanted to see what it was like. We also knew it was the furthest place we could drive to in the north of Canada, so it made sense to go there and visit it, and make that the main destination of our trip. Our second area for discovery was Alaska, although we really didn't know what to focus on or where we would go. Many of our friends had ideas for things for us to see and do, but since neither of us had really been to Alaska, wherever we went was fine with us.

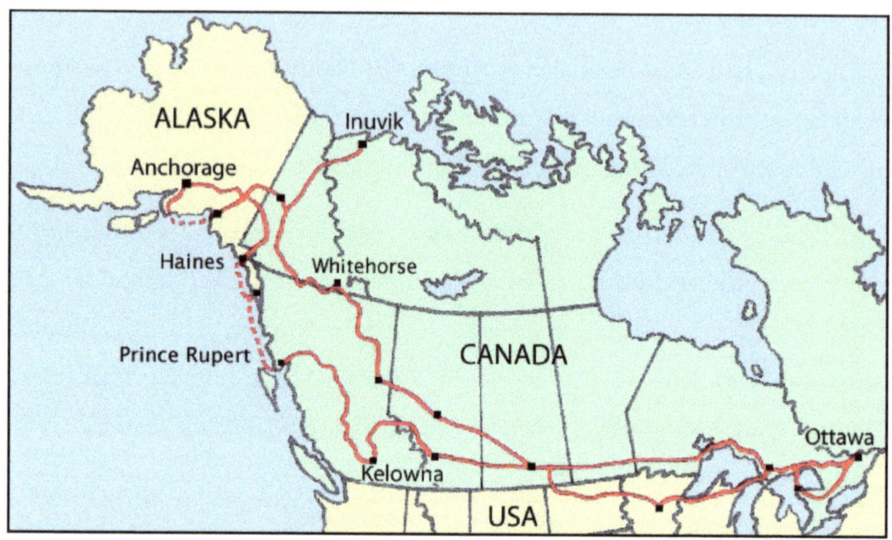

This is a map of our eventual travels. The fixed points were Inuvik, the ferry from Haines to Prince Rupert, Kelowna and our return to Ontario for the wedding

Cameras and computers with their chargers were packed away in their own cupboards; paperwork was all stashed away, including address labels for postcards to friends and family (especially grandchildren), passports, and health insurance. Maps and tourist information were stored in accessible spots for easy reference, the Garmin GPS was attached to the dashboard, and we were ready to go.

We were on our way, first west then north. The great adventure had begun.

OTTAWA CAMPING TRAILERS
SALES - SERVICE - PARTS - RENTALS
www.ottawacamping.ca

June 29th to July 2nd

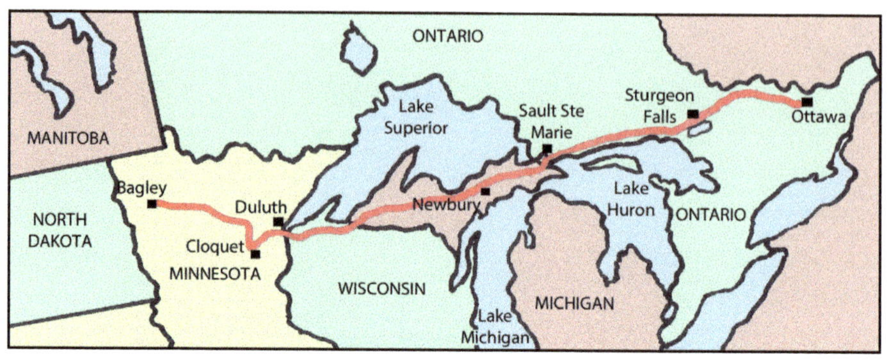

Ottawa to Sturgeon Falls	405km
Sturgeon Falls to Newbury	506km
Newbury to Cloquet	592km
Cloquet to Bagley	355km
TOTAL	1,858km

Chapter Three
The Start of the Trip: Ottawa to Bagley

We left on June 29th on a hot summer morning after quickly packing the last few items into the RV. The house was prepared for leaving—blinds drawn, electronics all switched off, windows closed, doors locked—and now after months of planning we were really on our way to Inuvik and anywhere else we chose to go.

It was hot but not too hot, and the roads were their usual selves. Highway 17 was rough between Deep River and Mattawa but this was good, because we were able to feel and hear just how well our packing stood up to the shaking and banging of the road. As we drove we remembered the comments friends of ours had made about this stretch of road. According to them, it was one of the worse roads they had driven during their trip to Inuvik. Bob and I laughed at the time, but as we drove over the lumps and bumps we thought about that comment.

Driving along Highway 17 brought back memories of our trip to Vancouver. We had taken courage in both hands and had driven our three children, ages eight, ten and twelve, off to Expo '86. At that time it was all about tenting, so we had packed the family and all the accoutrements needed for the trip into a very underpowered diesel Vanagon. That trip was wonderful and we all had a great time, but this time our travels were a lot more comfortable as we took our 'house' with us, and had the added advantage of a much more powerful engine (but with much enhanced fuel bills).

After a good day of driving we remembered that this was the Canada Day weekend, so as we drove into North Bay we checked in with the tourist information office, and the helpful staff called around and found us a spot in a campground in Sturgeon Falls. The campground was on Lake Nipissing, and after a refreshing swim in the lake we settled down to enjoy our first night on the road.

Lake Nipissing in the evening light

Our plan was to make it across the border and into Michigan the next day, so after a quick stop at the local bakery we started on our way. We were pleasantly surprised by the road, as it had been upgraded and repaired since our last trip in 1986. While it may seem strange that the Trans Canada is still not a four-lane highway, it now has very frequent and long passing zones, which allowed faster vehicles to pass us regularly and safely. (We maintain the speed limit in most zones, which means we are passed by almost everybody!)

Picnic near Sault Ste Marie

Lunch saw us in a picnic area near Sault Ste Marie. While there we met a nice young couple, with their two dogs and budgie, on the way to Ottawa where they were both planning to work. It was fun talking to them; he was from The Soo and she had originally come from Ottawa. Their rented van was filled to the roof with all their possessions, and they were towing their car, which was also full to the gunnels. Among their belongings there was a fish tank with water snails on the floor of the car, with the pump plugged into the cigarette lighter. Unfortunately, the tank had cracked en route, so the snails would need to find a new home when they arrived in Ottawa, doubtless provided by Kijiji. We wished the couple luck and admired the courage of two young people loading up everything they had in the world and heading off to a new life. Chance meetings, such as this, became a very pleasant hallmark of our travels.

Then it was on to the Michigan border. Since traveling with the RV we have learned the questions always asked by border guards, so now we give the answers before they ask: "We have no citrus, no raw meat, two bottles of wine, no tobacco, and no firearms." It makes for a quick crossing and so far we have not been searched! As always, our first stop was at the Michigan welcome centre for maps, campsite and tourist information, and anything else we thought would be helpful. This became one of the least interesting parts of our journey; the roads were not great and the scenery was generic; trees, bushes, swamps, forest, and very few amenities, including campgrounds. We were beginning to think we might have to find a motel—almost as rare as campgrounds—when I spotted a KOA (Kampgrounds of America) sign near Newbury, so with much squeaking on my part, we braked, turned in and found our campsite for the night.

In the past, as a family who prided themselves on tent camping on our long trips with young children, we would see KOAs advertized on the highways. As we drove past them we would look at all the RVs and trailers and smugly say, "That looks awful; we'll never stay there." How our youthful words come back to haunt us! We had truly discovered the usefulness of the KOA brand when we first drove down to Florida and stayed in one. We now realize how useful they are, and we tend to look for them on those long days of driving. We recognize them for dependable, clean campsites with the facilities we need. Are we converts? Yes, but for one or two nights only. As a good stopping spot for the night, or as a base for tourist excursions, a KOA is a great place. Because we like to keep moving we tend not to stay for much longer than two or three days. However, with all the amenities offered we can see the advantages they have for other visitors who may want to stay longer.

As we settled into our campsite, I noticed a strong smell of propane as I started to prepare supper. The main valve on the tank was leaking! After a few minutes of work with a wrench Bob realized that it needed more than just a quick fix. We managed to cook supper using the microwave and the barbeque, but knew we needed to find a licenced service place to do the repair work.

When we bought the RV it was recommended that we have a roadside service plan for the vehicle, so we settled on Coachman Roadside Assistance (CRA). We felt the company that had built the vehicle would be the best resource for servicing, and we found this was true during an earlier trip when a tire had been damaged. On that occasion CRA was very helpful and arranged to for us to have a service call, a tow and a replacement tire all for just the price of the tire. The plan had paid for the rest. So we made a call to CRA for advice on our propane tank. Once again they were very helpful and, since this was a Saturday, between us we were able to estimate our location on Sunday night and the location of a service station nearby on the Monday morning. Once we had arranged that small detail we were able to relax and enjoy the evening.

Canada Day saw us leaving Newbury and heading towards Duluth. We drove around the south shore of Lake Superior, which is incredibly beautiful, and then headed west again. And that's when we saw large bill boards advertising "Da Yoober's, the Largest Tourist Trap, free washrooms, free coffee." We laughed and kept going, and then came across the building! It was time to stop. It was so bad it was wonderful!

The beautiful south shore of Lake Superior

The Da Yoober's gift shop was the 'gift shop to end all gift shops', as tacky as they come. There were 'motto boards' everywhere, which ranged from very sexist comments to some rather amusing ones. I really enjoyed one since it resonated with my love of birds and bird feeders: "You give the birds seeds and they poop on your deck." The postcards too, were varied, some off-the-wall in the bad taste department, while others were the traditional scenic kind. Likewise the ball caps, T-shirts, sweatshirts, etc. The free coffee was there, but we didn't dare try it! It might have been very good, but we will never know. Outside the building were weird and wonderful sculptures, if you could call them that: a pickup truck with a huge wooden rifle on top, models of local events with strange looking dummies sitting in boats, wagons, bicycles, and so on. Totally bizarre, it had to be seen to be believed. It truly was the tourist trap of all time! However, we didn't buy anything!

The roadside symbol for Da Yoobers says it all

Since it was July 1st I was wearing my Canada Day T-shirt, and as we left the store a voice called out "Happy Canada Day." We chatted for a few minutes with the family who had greeted us, and learned that they were also from Ontario. We were both happy to have this day acknowledged when away from home.

After we left Da Yoobers we looked for a nice picnic spot for lunch, and found a lovely shaded area overlooking a lake, with all the amenities one could want. We enjoyed a quiet lunch under the trees, and then checked out the washrooms. Now we had a dilemma. The outside wall of the washroom area had the labels Men and Women. So far so good, but behind the wall on the actual washrooms the labels were reversed, so it was Women and Men! Which to use? Given the ambiguity of it all, we felt it didn't matter, so in we went. Inside the usual graffiti in both washrooms was written by men for men about men! It was certainly different from the graffiti I was used to, but for Bob it was quite normal! I guess I don't usually see the inside of the men's washrooms!

As we traveled further down the road, we were stopped by a traffic jam which we thought unusual. The traffic was at a complete standstill and nothing was moving in either direction, so after a few minutes Bob went to investigate. It was a 4th of July parade on July 1st crossing a major intersection. Bob watched the parade while I stayed with the RV.

Scenes from the parade that closed the highway

While I was sitting in the vehicle the horses, which had been part of the parade, passed right in front of me, and I thought this was the best part of the whole experience. Once the parade was over and we were moving again it was time to decide where we would stay that evening. We had passed through Michigan and Wisconsin, and would soon be in Minnesota. The distance initially looked daunting until we realized how narrow these states really are when compared with Ontario.

Eventually we found a KOA in Cloquet, Minnesota. While we were relaxing in the pool we started a conversation with another couple. They were from Washington State and had been traveling on a Harley-Davidson towing a trailer. Now they were on their way back home, having spent time in Niagara Falls. He had loved motorbikes as long as he could remember, and now their kids were older the freedom of the road beckoned. Bob and he compared V-twin engines, and Bob described his 1929 Morgan three wheeler (below). The conversation drifted to wine and an interesting discussion ensued on the products of Washington State and the Okanagan Valley, where some of Canada's best wines are produced.

After our swim and supper it was time to prepare for the morning when we would get the propane tank fixed. July 2nd was a day to remember! CRA had referred us to Oak Lake Campground, which also had an approved repair shop, so that was our first destination. There had been a little rain the evening before, so just before we left we extended the awning to dry. Having been RVing for two years, we felt confident in getting the van ready for leaving without using checklists! Big mistake! Water and electric disconnected and stowed away, *check*; leveling blocks put away, *check*; all doors properly closed, *check*; bathroom door open and clipped back, *check*; all loose stuff properly tidied away, *check*; Lets go! As I drove through the campground there was a nasty noise as if a large bush or small tree was brushing against the side! Unfortunately, it wasn't the side of the camper; as we discovered when I stopped and got out, it was the awning! Yes, the awning was damaged, and so was the tree, the only difference being, the tree would recover on its own, while the awning would need work. So after closing it as best we could, we were off to the repair shop. And, yes, as supposedly seasoned RVers we find it takes some courage to put this incident in print.

Fortunately the repair shop was only about 25 minutes away, so I gingerly drove the van down the road, grateful that these were slower roads with lower speed limits. Even so, I could hear the wind as it went whistling through and around the damaged awning fittings. We arrived at Oak Lake campground and located the repair shop in the grounds. After speaking to the owner and the service manager about the leak, they assured us they would be able to fix it and get us back on the road.

So we left them to sort it all out. First the propane tank had to be vented before the dysfunctional valve could be replaced. The vehicle was moved to an open space, the valve was then fully opened and the gas released. It sounded like a rocket engine taking off, but without the flame! We watched as a huge cloud of white pulsating gas shot out of the tank and saw shock waves moving in the cloud. While this process only took a couple of minutes it left a lasting impression on both of us. Throughout this process we had started chatting to another customer, and he and Bob had set about repairing the awning with a few borrowed tools. It was a very hot and humid day and the RV was in full sunlight, which may have partially explained what happened next. They released a bolt and thanks to the hydraulic system in the awning mechanism, the awning arm sprung up and now the strut wouldn't go back into its proper alignment. At this point the RV was brought back to the service area where the replacement of the valve was done. Then the service manager and one of his strong men climbed onto the roof and, with brute force and Bob's help, were able to get the awning strut into the right place and put a bolt in to secure it! It was hard work, but done in a remarkably short time. Soon everything was secured and we went on our way again after paying about $200.00, which we thought very reasonable given the circumstances. We would recommend the kind and helpful people of Oak Lake Campground, Minnesota to anyone passing through the region.

We continued west along Highway 2 and crossed a tiny creek passing under the road. I noticed this little creek was named the Mississippi River! We both laughed since we have a Mississippi River not far from us in Ontario, and then we started wondering if these were in fact the head-waters of the Great Mississippi. It called for further investigation so out came the map, and we were able to trace the river north from the Mississippi River Delta to its headwaters in Minnesota. We really had driven over the Mississippi in its infancy.

After this rather busy day we stopped in a little town called Bagley. It was very hot and humid and the manager of the campsite commented that it was unusually hot for the time of year, and that they needed rain because it was so dry. The campsite was situated on an inviting lake so we went for a relaxing swim. This proved to be anything but relaxing as we watched the clouds rapidly thickening up in the west, with thunder and lightning closing in on the lake.

The storm was moving fast towards us, the swimming area was emptying just as fast, and we followed suit! The storm arrived so quickly that it was on us before we knew it. When it hit the RV things became quite scary. It was as dark as night, something I have never before experienced during a storm. The RV was shaking in the wind gusts, and we suddenly felt how vulnerable we were. It made us think about the various disasters we had heard about befalling RVs in storms! Then came the hail and the rain, which hit the roof and sides of the vehicle with a tremendous noise. The trees were being tossed by the wind and rain, and the thunder and lightning were almost continuous. And the rain! It was torrential, and although we were parked about 100 metres from the lake, we could barely see it. What we could see of the lake was exciting but not comforting. It was a maelstrom of waves moving in every direction, while the rain created floods everywhere, including a 'new' river running under our RV. We kept thanking our lucky stars we weren't in tents! Eventually, the wind began to drop, but the rain continued to come back in waves, each time a little less strong, until it finally stopped about an hour after the storm had initially hit us. There was a continual rumbling of thunder and flashes of lightning as the disturbance moved eastwards. Finally, when it had mostly blown out, we were able to eat our supper. After that we went outside, as did many others in the campground, and took a walk to look around. We learned from one of the other campers that the wind gusts were up to 62 miles per hour. No wonder the vehicle shook. As we watched, the lake became a mirror just reflecting the sunset, with no sign of the turbulence we had seen before. It amazed us to see how quickly things appeared to get back to normal.

The storm passes through the campsite leaving a beautiful sunset

July 3rd to July 7th

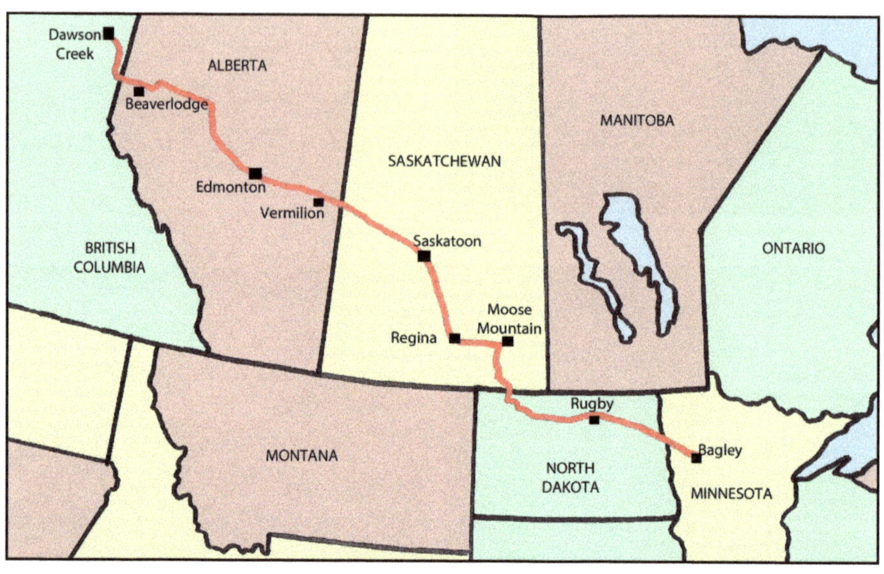

Bagley to Moose Mountain	772km
Moose Mountain to Regina	246km
Regina to Vermilion	630km
Vermilion to Beaverlodge	696km
Beaverlodge to Dawson Creek	90km
TOTAL	2,434km

Chapter Four
Bagley to Dawson Creek

After we had recovered from the storm in Bagley we began to plan our return to Canada. It was now the eve of July 4th, which was a concern as we anticipated traffic holdups on the following day (if previous experience was anything to go by). So after an early start, we drove across the border into North Dakota where we made our usual visit to the welcome centre to get maps for us and postcards for the grandchildren.

We found an attractive roadside picnic shelter where we paused for lunch. While we sat in the shelter a very upset swallow started flying around us. After a few minutes of this I stood up, looked around the roof beams, and found her nest with baby birds in it. Even though we didn't actually see the babies, the swallow's agitation indicated they were there, so we got up, moved outside and sat on the ground! Now the bird no longer bothered us, and we were left to have our lunch in peace. An indication of how far west we had come was a yellow-headed blackbird wandering in the grass and weeds. It reminded us of that long-ago trip to Expo '86, when we had seen them for the first time.

As we drove towards the Canadian border we saw much evidence of flooding. We could see that the water behind levees was several feet above land level, and there were ponds left in the fields from earlier flooding, along with a variety of man-made objects sitting in the middle of the flooded fields. It reminded us of the flooding we had read about in the spring, and gave us a better understanding of the devastation those floods caused.

As we traveled further west we came upon the small city of Rugby, whose claim to fame is the assertion that it is geographical centre of North America. There was a small monument in its honour, but we did wonder how they came to decide this particular location!

Rugby's claim to fame

Finally, we were at the US/Canada border, which we passed with no difficulty. So after a quick stop at the welcome center we booked a campsite in Moose Mountain Provincial Park. We were very tired at this point and didn't look at the map very closely. It didn't take long to realize the park was nearly 100 km away, and we were driving straight into those proverbial prairie winds! However, the park itself was well worth seeing, and we enjoyed our brief sojourn there.

We had now been on the road for almost a week. After a restful night in the park we drove to Regina, about two hours away, and found the Comfort Plus campsite, which had the bonus of being close to a big box store plaza. We happily spent the day shopping, cooking, doing laundry and scraping off the bugs covering the front of the vehicle, thus making it look much more presentable.

Later in the evening we wandered through the campsite, met a gentleman from Whitehorse, and inevitably started chatting. We spoke of our plans to drive to Inuvik, so out came the horror stories: 'razor sharp' shale that slashes tires better than a knife, barriers telling you the road is closed, ferries washed out, bugs the size of sparrows that bite through your clothing, etc. However, as the conversation proceeded he began to realize that we had actually done our homework, had read *The Milepost* and had planned the trip carefully. His tune changed considerably and he became a mine of useful information. Although a Winnipegger, he had fallen in love with the Yukon (like so many others) and had moved to Whitehorse. Among his pursuits was time-keeping for the Yukon Quest, one of the most challenging sled dog races, and one which puts the more famous Iditarod to shame. Bob reminisced of the time he was lucky to be in Dawson City on the day the Yukon Quest came through.

It was so pleasant and fortunate to find someone who understood our plans and knew the route, and was happy to share his knowledge. As we walked back to the RV we did have a moment of two of panic, thinking about his dire but modified warnings and wondered what we were thinking! Then we remembered our friends, Hazel and Byron (*RV-ing and Other Adventures North of 60*) who had driven to Inuvik without too much difficulty, and they were at least 10 years older than us, and were pulling a trailer! Those thoughts reassured us for a little while, but we realized then, as we started heading north, that our planned adventures were likely to provide unexpected challenges, and hoped we were up to dealing with them.

The enormous horizon and the brilliant yellow canola

We left early the next day, and quickly found ourselves driving through cattle farming areas. The horizon became enormous, with the many farms glowing with the yellow of the rape seed (canola). We realized how dependent we are on our farmers and how infrequently we think of them. There was so much large equipment on dealer's lots: rows and rows of tractors, seeders, irrigators, etc., a stark reminder of the cost of farming and the debt-load so many farmers carry. Now, when I am in the grocery, I think about that cost and don't complain so much about the prices! The other side of farming was also noticeable: the properties that looked decrepit and rundown, perhaps abandoned, and near the cities new housing developments built on what used to be farmland.

A typical oil pump in the middle of farm fields

We were interested to see some farmers 'growing' oil nodding donkeys in their fields, which are used to pump low volumes of oil from the ground. It likely adds to the farmers' income and no doubt helps to pay the bills.

As we drove we were fascinated with the sky; it was huge and blue, with white puffy clouds. And then as we focused on the sky, the topography would suddenly change! The land appeared flat to the horizon, and then without warning a valley would open up and a river could be seen flowing along the bottom. Equally suddenly the valley would disappear and the horizon would be level once more. It was as if a magician had waved his wand to make us see all these changes as we drove through the area. And now, finally in Saskatchewan, there was a little more wildlife; we spotted a couple of coyotes quietly walking around in the fields and across the roads. Not a great deal of wildlife, but more than we had seen for a while.

As always, our RV was thirsty, necessitating a gas stop break that gave us the opportunity to make a quick visit to the local diner. There we met an older lady in an adjacent booth who was nursing a cup of coffee. As we sat down with our drinks she initiated the conversation by asking where we were from. As we started chatting she changed booths to be closer to us. She talked of the restaurants closing in the town, and the general depression due to the unpredictable weather. This was a theme we would hear a lot: discussing the weather is a nice neutral subject and easy to talk around, but now it seemed we heard much more than usual about extreme events, and of course we described the massive storm we had experienced just a few days previously. As we left, the older lady went off to the counter for a fill-up, no doubt hoping to find someone else to talk to. Was this her way of filling her day; just meeting new people as they came into the diner for a coffee break?

During the early part of this trip we had always tried to find attractive places to stop and make lunch, but on this day we decided to try out one of the many roadside restaurants. So we checked one out, and a very nice change it was too, until... As I was leaving the restaurant I tripped and fell. Knowing my proclivity for twisting my ankles, I assumed that was all I had done. However, it became very clear that a trip to hospital in Vermilion, Alberta was in order! And, yes, a small bone was broken! Visions of turning round and heading back home haunted me until the doctor informed me that I would not need a cast, and that if I treated it carefully I would certainly be able to dance at our niece's wedding in August. That made all the difference, and we went to the campsite, not very happy but at least knowing that we could continue our trip. This incident made me value the importance of the Canadian healthcare system. I had hurt myself in Saskatchewan, was examined in Alberta and the treatment was paid for by Ontario. For all the complaints we hear about healthcare, I could only say thank you, and be grateful that this had not happened in the United States, even with the insurance we carried.

Later that evening we went for a very short walk around the campsite and stopped to chat with our neighbours at the next site. The two guys were drivers for the oil industry, and the woman with them was the partner of one of them. This trio traveled wherever there was work to be had; they had a large trailer and found that campsites were an economical place to stay while they were working. The distances they traveled with their pickup trucks put our trip into diminished perspective. These are the solid, hardworking people we rely to keep our Ford RV fueled in trips across this great country. Their vehicles are a testament to the work they do; a stark contrast to those precious chromed and carpeted pick-ups we frequently see in the city.

The next morning it was off to Vegreville where the largest *pysanka* (Ukrainian Easter egg) in the world is to be found. Apparently, the Queen had dedicated the egg and the park in 1978. As I sat in the middle of this lovely, peaceful place and watched the ducks, I wondered what she must have thought at the time, and does she still remember it?

As we drove northwest, we noticed the farmland was giving way to forest, and we started to imagine what the next few days would bring. We hoped to reach Dawson Creek early the following day; Mile Zero of the Alaska Highway and the official start of our adventures up North.

What must the Queen have thought? The geese don't seem to mind

The road we were on had some lovely rest areas. At one such stop, Bob met a couple from South Carolina who were also going north, and he discussed our travel plans and learned they were heading towards the Mackenzie River side of the Northwest Territories, before driving to Alaska. Meanwhile, I met a lady with a sore knee and we commiserated with each other. Her destination was Yellowknife, and she spoke briefly about her trip to Inuvik a few years previously and recommended a great train trip she had taken from Whitehorse to Skagway. This sounded so good that Bob and I planned to check into this when we arrived in Whitehorse.

It had been a long day's driving so when we found ourselves in a funny little campsite just off the highway in a place called Beaverlodge we were happy to stop! But far from relaxing, Bob had to set to work on the RV. He discovered that a seam on the roof panels above the cab had opened, and all the insulation was exposed to the elements! Having something like this happen, we were glad to be in campground with a very helpful manager and his very good toolkit. With much struggling and swearing, Bob was able to get the loose piece tucked back under the strip that was supposed to hold it in place, then with caulking and multiple screws (thanks to the manager) and several long strips of duct tape, the job was done! It was pretty clear to us that the rough roads we had encountered, particularly in Ontario and Michigan, had contributed to this failure. When we returned to Ottawa after our trip, Coachmen was glad to underwrite the cost of repairs; another example of the excellent service we have had from the company. Now to see if the repair would hold up on the Dempster Highway...

A repair to the roof. This turned out to be good practice for other little problems we might encounter en route.

Putting aside the difficulties with the roof the previous night, we woke up early because we were so excited that we would finally get to Dawson Creek and the start of the Alaska Highway.

We drove into Dawson Creek early, stopped for gas and spent a few interesting minutes talking with the gas jockey. He was a Grade 10 student and had just returned from a school trip to Montreal and Quebec

City and was eager to tell us his plans for the future. He just loved gaming and graphic arts and hoped it would become a career, so he had been checking out software companies and schools in various locations. It may be just a dream, but with dreams like that he might just succeed. We could only wish him well, and maybe one day we'll hear about a guy from Dawson Creek doing some amazing graphics. After filling up it was time to visit the tourist centre and learn all we could about the next part of the trip.

July 7th to July 9th

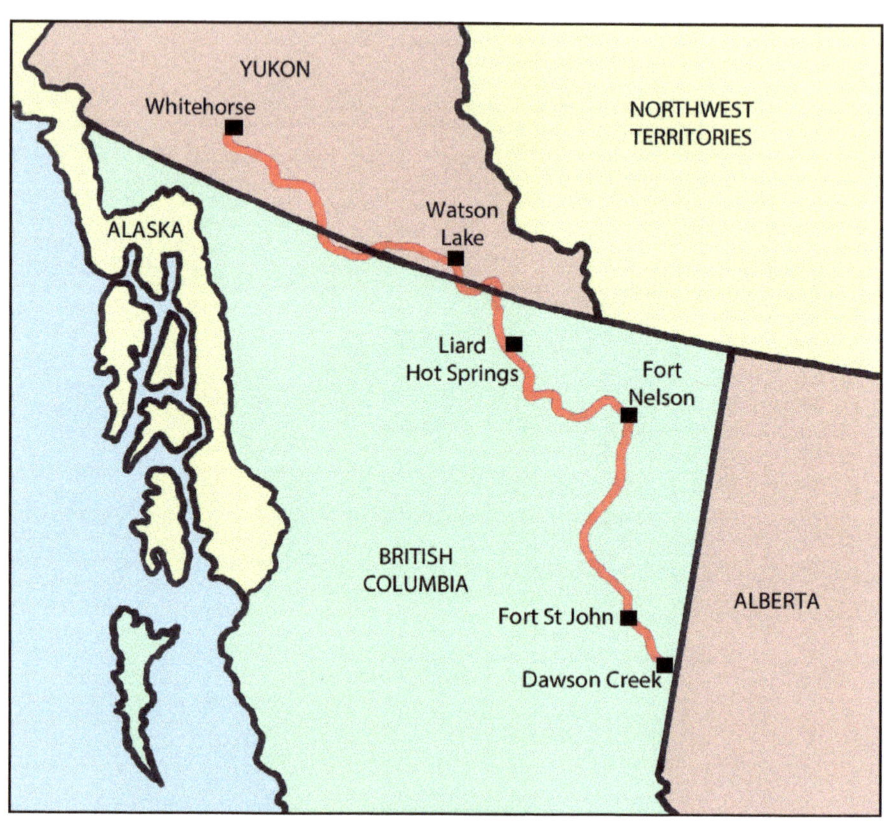

Dawson Creek to Fort Nelson	351km
Fort Nelson to Liard Hot Springs	301km
Liard Hot Springs to Whitehorse	641km
TOTAL	1,293km

Chapter Five

Dawson Creek to Whitehorse

The visitor centre in Dawson Creek is housed in the Northern Alberta Railway Station Museum, which makes it a very interesting place to visit. We spent some time in the original railway booking office and, along with many other visitors, checked and responded to emails, while appreciating the contrast between the old booking office and the present day use of WiFi! After talking to the staff of the visitor centre we found all our earlier preparations had provided us with most of the information needed for the next part of our trip. Then we wandered around the museum and appreciated the exhibits that depicted the early times of the area.

There was a dental chair on display in the museum, and after our return home we spoke to a distant family member who had actually sat in it when she was there in the 1940s. We enjoyed her very acerbic comments about the dentist of that period. Finally, before leaving the visitor centre we sent the traditional souvenir postcards of Mile Zero to the family, just to remind them of how far we had traveled.

Now we had to actually find Mile Zero of the Alaska Highway so we could start our further exploration. We quickly found the marker a short distance away from the museum and took the requisite picture. After all, if there was no picture, were we really there?

Mile Zero, the true start of the adventure to the North

When we started this journey I had little idea of the history of the Alaska Highway and its importance to both Canada and the United States. I finally learned the history of this important road link when we were in Juneau, Alaska on our way back home. Much to my surprise I found that the Alaska Highway was built in 1942 by the US Army, following the

Japanese invasion of the Aleutian Islands. This route, passing through Canada, was the only way Alaska could be connected to the rest of the United States. It took nine months of hard labour by the military, and initially was a mud and gravel road just designed to allow military transports to carry troops and supplies into the north. For some years the highway was only used by the military, but in 1948 it was opened for general use and paved a little while later. Even though the road has been paved there are frequent washouts along its length, which makes it challenging for the unprepared driver.

As we left Dawson Creek we wondered about the condition of the road, given all the stories we had heard about driving in the North; tales of washouts, narrow roads, crazy drivers, to name but a few. So we were pleasantly surprised to find the highway was just like any other highway; initially a very reasonable four-lane road, but soon narrowing down to two lanes. We were stunned by the scenery and kept pointing out new, different and wonderful sights; so much more that we had anticipated. Then at one point the foothills of the Rockies could be seen in the distance, which just emphasized how far we had traveled.

The further we drove the more we found that this was not a flat road! There are lots of serious hills and on this, our first day of driving, we learned all about them. Traveling these hills, while they were beautiful, was not relaxing; the roads were not straight, and going down these steep and winding inclines was an ongoing challenge; very reminiscent of the roads in the Alps in Europe. It became quite a predictable pattern; down, down, down to river level, over a narrow bridge, and up, up, up the mountain. We did this so often that first day it became our mantra for driving. At one point traffic was stopped by a 'lollipop man' at the top of a hill, because the construction people were hard at work repairing the road. (It reminded me a little of driving in Ottawa in the summer with the all the construction we see there.) This was our first experience of road construction in the North and, as we later discovered, was not unusual. Much to our surprise we had to wait for a long time which did allow for some photography.

Road repairs were a common sight as we continued north

We came across the Peace River—which is huge even this far from its mouth—and numerous smaller rivers. These rivers had created amazing erosion patterns in their valleys; very different from anything we had seen before.

By the afternoon we noticed the scenery had changed somewhat, with lots of black spruce, reminding us of our train ride to Moosonee several years previously, passing though acres of those trees that make up the Northern Ontario landscape. We had been warned about wildlife and the risk posed to traffic, but surprisingly we saw little evidence of it as we drove along; one deer on the side of the road, and one very dead moose! We were disappointed because we had been looking forward to seeing northern fauna throughout our travels.

The Peace River valley

We were now beginning to appreciate the real benefit of *The Milepost.* It directed us to a campground near Fort Nelson where we enjoyed its Wild West theme. Unlike so many of the campgrounds we had visited in the past, this one had a restaurant and a take-out menu, which was a pleasant surprise. We took advantage of that service and bought dessert from the camp store: Black Forest cheesecake; delicious.

As we left Fort Nelson in the morning the first thing we saw on the highway was an illuminated sign warning of bison on the road. This was a new way of indicating some of the risks this road might pose for the unwary traveler, and very different from our other travels further south.

We didn't see any bison for most of the day, and were feeling a little disappointed until finally we saw one just before we stopped for the night. After all, we had only ever seen them before in the controlled setting of a wildlife park.

The Wild West theme of our campground in Fort Nelson

We noticed some interesting driving demonstrated by motorists on this highway. They seemed to think the normal rules of the road were merely guidelines. So, speed limits were just a suggestion, passing on a curve with double yellow lines is fine, and who needs turn signals? It made for some interesting and somewhat hairy moments. Like the time when Bob was driving on a very bendy piece of road and wanted to make a left turn into a look-off. So after signaling and checking behind, he turned into the look-off and was hit by a car whose driver was trying to pass on an outside curve with a double yellow line! Fortunately, the damage was very minor and after the usual exchange of information, we were on our way again. Thankfully this was the last of our mini-disasters of the trip, although it would have been nice to know that at the time.

Later on that day we found a restaurant and gas station which advertised the best cinnamon buns on the highway. That required a stop, both for gas and to make sure the cinnamon buns were indeed the best on the highway. So we checked it out! It also gave us the opportunity to notify the RCMP about our minor accident. Fortunately, the restaurant also had cell coverage, a service not found along most of the Alaska Highway. I was able to contact the RCMP and I was told that if the cars were drivable and no one was hurt, they did not take a report and just referred us to our insurance company. We realized we were now in a really different world from the one we knew! And, yes, we did enjoy the best cinnamon buns on the highway!

The cinnamon buns lived up to the hype

Finally we came across Stone Mountain sheep on the road beside Muncho Lake. They were on the side of the road and wandering across it.

We took a couple of minutes out, watched them and took pictures. Then, on looking around we realized they were everywhere. The sides of the mountain seemed totally barren, which made us wonder what they found to eat. I guessed they were used to eating the very sparse vegetation found on the mountain and near the lake.

Stone Mountain sheep disrupting traffic

We drove beside Muncho Lake for some time, a very beautiful, large and long lake. The road had become flat and sinuous as it followed the shoreline, lacking any guardrails and having only a little section of gravel between us and the lake. The views were stunning; the beauty of the lake and mountains far outweighed the lack of security.

Distant views of the Rocky Mountains

The scenery was so interesting we would stop regularly to enjoy the views. On one such stop, overlooking one of the many rivers, another vehicle stopped, and we started chatting. Ton and Annika were from the Netherlands and were driving a great big military-looking rig built by VW/Mann, with living accommodations and other accoutrements especially designed by them. They had already traveled through North Africa, Pakistan, Iran and India, and were now heading for Alaska, north from Fairbanks to Prudhoe Bay on the Arctic Ocean. This would be followed by a trip through the western US, into Mexico and thence to Central and South America. And we thought *we* were adventurous.

Our hoped-for destination that day was Liard Hot Springs Provincial Park. We wanted to bathe in the springs, so when we checked-in we asked how far they were from the campsite. Fortunately for me, there is a golf cart service provided for decrepit campers, as I still had some discomfort from my injured foot. Everyone else has to use the boardwalk. We happily took advantage of the ride and went for a bathe in the very sulphurous and very hot spring. There were two pools, very hot and merely hot. After about an hour of total bliss, we were picked up by the golf cart and taken back to our campsite.

This is the lower pool; the upper one was far too hot for bathing

On our way to the springs we chatted with the driver of the golf cart. He and his girlfriend, who we had already met at the registration desk, were from Toronto. They were just completing their courses at York University in Environmental Studies, and Liard Hot Springs was their summer job. He spoke about the differences living at the Provincial Park; digging his own septic system for his trailer, rigging up a solar cell charger for his internet, and working out ways of providing clean, potable water. Hearing this we appreciated the luxury our RV provided.

As the weather was nice we decided to eat outside and thus met our first serious mosquitoes. Out came our easy-to-set-up dining tent and we enjoyed a relatively mosquito free dinner. We had now driven far enough north to realize that the days were becoming noticeably longer, and we were starting to wake up earlier and earlier. It was time to add the extra layer of curtains, made so many weeks ago, in preparation for this. These extra curtains meant we slept until about 6:30am instead of the 4:00am we had been experiencing so far. We left Liard Hot Springs early because we were looking forward to getting to Watson Lake and the famous Sign Post Forest.

The early start gave us the opportunity to see much more wildlife beside the road, an unexpected bonus. I was driving when Bob became very excited because he had seen a bear just 'being' on the side of the road. This was a first for him; he had only seen bears in captivity and to see one just ambling along looking for food was really exciting. After a quick, but careful pause for pictures we went on our way.

The first of many bears we saw that day

As we continued driving we kept encountering bears on the grassy sides of the road foraging for food. By the time number 11 showed up we were becoming almost blasé about it. We did catch a glimpse of a bear cub, who quickly ran back into the forest, probably to its mother. There were many buffalo just either sitting or grazing on the grass by the road, but we really didn't believe the *Milepost* when it said they would wander all over the road. Then, as we came around a bend we met a herd doing just that. Somewhat unwisely, we pulled over to take some pictures and walked toward the herd (which is not recommended) and after a few minutes the big bull spooked. With him leading them, the buffalo started to wander across the road, away from us but unfortunately towards the RV. So we hurried back and drove carefully around the herd. It was a wonderful experience to be so close to these magnificent creatures.

Buffalo occupying the road and just asking to be photographed

We continued to see buffalo beside the road, but only in small groups of one or two, rather than in a herd. Beaver lodges and their owners could be seen in the streams and lakes, while the bears continued to show themselves until we got to Watson Lake.

Watson Lake is famous for its Sign Post Forest. This tradition was initially started by a US serviceman, working on the Alaska Highway, who put up a sign with his name and the distance to his home. The practice has continued to this day and the signs now number over 17,000! Not to be outdone we added our name to the forest. Unfortunately we didn't bring a ready-made sign, but the local Home Hardware was well prepared for forgetful visitors and conveniently stocked pieces of 'just the right size' board for sale. We bought a board and went to the visitors centre near the Forest to borrow paints and a brush. Like the Home Hardware store, the visitors centre was also well prepared for forgetful visitors. Bob created a sign and we nailed it up in the middle of all the others, knowing that it would be cared for by the people of Watson Lake.

Lasting fame in Watson Lake

Once we had made our mark in the Sign Post forest, we decided we would be able to make it to Whitehorse by the mid-afternoon. The scenery along the way continued to be fantastic and we saw many large and looming mountains, nearly all bald, wide lakes and extremely large rivers. As we crossed the Continental Divide, where the water on one side flows to the Arctic and the other goes to the Pacific we commented on the distance these rivers would have to go before they arrived at their destination, and were curious to see, or at least find out, just how big they would become before decanting into the ocean.

We finally arrived in Whitehorse where we found a nice campground but, sadly, also noticed several campgrounds that were no longer open. Later on we understood why: all the RVs and trailers parking for free in the Walmart parking lot. We felt sad that campgrounds were going out of business because of this.

Once parked at our site and sorted out, it was time to touch base with our friends in Whitehorse, and make arrangements to join them the next morning.

July 10th to July 12th

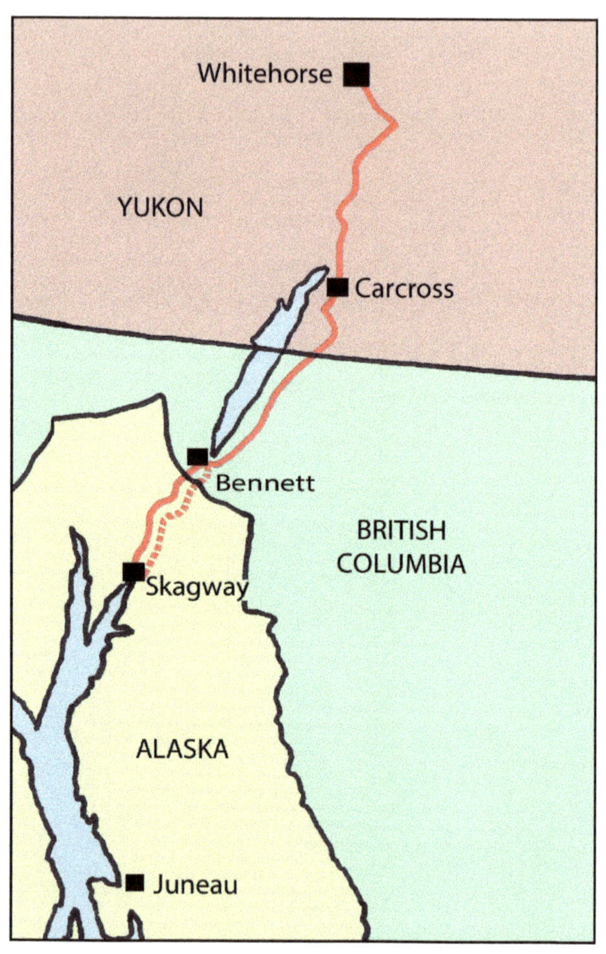

Whitehorse to Fraser (bus)	141km
Fraser to Skagway (train)	40km
Skagway to Whitehorse (bus)	282km
TOTAL	463km

Chapter Six
Whitehorse and Skagway

After a restful night, we left the campsite and drove to the house of Bob's friend and colleague Mike Gates. But before we parked the RV in his driveway, there were a couple of things to do first. The vehicle was in dire need of a wash and bug removal, the story of its life in the North. Bob was responsible for that little task, while my job was to buy a beautiful bracelet made in the Yukon, which would complement my outfit for the wedding. The bracelet was also a lovely souvenir of our trip and has been worn several times.

Mike and his family live in the Porter Creek subdivision, just outside Whitehorse, and when we arrived there in the late morning we met Mike's wife Kathy who is very busy working on a biography of Martha and George Black, Yukon personalities, pioneers and politicians from the early days. We learned a lot from her about the Blacks and their huge influence on the Yukon. We also met Mike and Kathy's daughter Megan, who makes finely crafted greeting cards, and her fiancé Richard Brandvold.

Bob and Mike were colleagues at the Canadian Conservation Institute (CCI) in Ottawa in the mid 1970s, and they had stayed in touch after Mike move to Dawson City and subsequently to Whitehorse while working for Parks Canada. Mike is retired now and spends much of his time researching, lecturing and writing books about the history and character of the Yukon. He also produces a weekly column for the

Yukon News containing vignettes of the area's history and characters.

As with many of our longer breaks, we spent the first morning in Whitehorse doing those annoying chores in the RV that never seem to go away. As we walked across the parking lot to Canadian Tire to acquire some more wing mirrors and another roll of duct tape (among other things) we met Ton and Annika again. Their rig was so different for the rest of the RVs and trailers in the parking lot that it was hard to miss. We chatted for a few minutes and heard about some of the difficulties they had encountered. They were staying in Whitehorse for a couple of days before continuing their travels to Alaska.

The Barclays (left) and the Gates' and Brandvold (right)

Whitehorse has a very attractive Waterfront Trolley which travels beside the Yukon River. We both thought it looked fun so we took this novel ride from terminus to terminus, a distance of about 4 km. The electric trolley runs on 36″ gauge tracks, some of which follow the original White

Pass and Yukon Route, and judging by the lettering inside the car it was originally used in either Spain or Portugal. The tracks are not electrified so the little trolley pulls or pushes its own power car, a diesel engine and generator mounted on a tiny four-wheeled bogie. The whole assembly rattles and crashes along in fine style. The best part of the ride was the stop in the 'roundhouse' (which wasn't round) to repair an oil pan loosened by the vibration. While this was being done, Bob and I looked at an exhibition of photographs about the building of the railroad over the White Pass. This was really interesting as this was the route we would be taking by train to Skagway the following day. With the repair to the oil pan almost completed, the engineer asked around the trolley crew for duct tape. To their amusement we answered, "We have some if you need it." Fortunately, they had some handy so didn't need ours. I really believe this world would stop functioning without the Handyman's Secret Weapon! Then it was time to continue our ride to the end of the line. There are several trolley stops, one of which is the original White Pass and Yukon Route train station. This station has been preserved and is now used as a booking office for the scenic train trip to Skagway on the narrow gauge White Pass and Yukon Route Railway; the trip we had heard about in Saskatchewan and were now ready to enjoy.

We had a very pleasant evening with our friends, talking and reminiscing about times gone by. They kindly volunteered to get us to the rail station bright and early the next morning.

We arrived at the rail station feeling very excited and looking forward to the trip. This is one of the most spectacular mountain railways in the world. Originally it ran from Skagway all the way to Whitehorse, but the track now only extends to Carcross, Yukon, so a bus takes passengers from the station in Whitehorse to the train. Our train started in Fraser, British Columbia, where we boarded for the last 40km or so down to Skagway, the most spectacular portion of the trip. There is an option of leaving from Carcross—nearer to Whitehorse—but unfortunately those trains were fully booked, so we had to take the shorter train trip. Our train was hauled by diesels; steam-hauled trains run twice a week but, again, these had been fully booked for months.

The bus left Whitehorse station at 8:30 and an hour later arrived in Carcross. The town apparently acquired its name from the original Caribou Crossing when the local bishop kept losing his mail due to the number of Caribou Crossings in the region. He requested that the name become *Car* (from the Caribou) and *Cross* (from the Crossing). This request was honoured and one hopes that the bishop then received all his mail.

Spirit Lake, one of the most photographed in the Yukon

The route the bus followed was mostly forest and low hills until we came to Spirit Lake where a beautiful vista of the Montana mountain group opened out before us. Spirit Lake was a beautiful turquoise colour due to calcium-rich microorganisms in the water, and is one of the most frequently photographed lakes in the Yukon. We stopped for coffee in Carcross and enjoyed an excellent raspberry scone in a newly-opened sourdough bakery. There was some time for exploring, so we briefly visited the terminal buildings of the railway, saw the little 0-6-0 locomotive *Countess* displayed outside, and viewed a girder bridge that carries the railroad across the river at that point. Then it was back onto the bus to Fraser, British Columbia.

Carcross station and the bridge across the river

At this point the northern part of British Columbia forms a panhandle over Alaska, so going south from Whitehorse you cross into British Columbia, and then cross the Alaska border just north of Skagway. Later on we learned that during the Klonidike era Canada's North-West Mounted Police were stationed at the three passes into the gold fields: the Chilkoot, the White and the Chilkat. In 1903 these posts were used to define the international border, which explains the territorial geography of this region.

After Carcross the scenery became much more grandiose with lots of views of snow-capped mountains and lakes. Our train was waiting for us at Fraser and we boarded car No. 266. There were 14 cars on this train, all but one of the old clerestory pattern, and each beautifully paneled in varnished wood and equipped with a woodstove. The seatbacks could be flipped over so the seats could face in either direction.

Car No. 266 (left) the woodstove (below) and an interior view showing the fine woodwork

To say the trip is spectacular is to undersell it; the rail line winds along the edges of mountainsides, cuts into the rock, and weaves in sharp curves. The 36″ gauge track crosses trestles and bridges, plunges into tunnels, and descends from the White Pass summit at almost 900m to sea level, at a remarkable 3.9% grade. At one point in a long loop, a train that left half an hour before ours could be seen clinging to the rock a kilometre across the valley.

Views from the train

There were two locomotives hauling our train, and after the brief climb to the summit just south of Fraser, all they did was provide braking for the descent. One could stand outside the car on the balconies at each end, and this was a really exhilarating experience as there was nothing between you and the deep gorge below, except a number of train buffs with cameras, included several wearing striped engineer's hats.

Skagway is now a cruise ship town and is filled with many gift shops selling gold, silver and precious stones; a far cry from the Klondike era, when it would be full of men hoping to make their fortune in the goldfields. Exceptions were the odd shop that wasn't entirely filled with items aimed at tourists.

The main street of Skagway with a docked cruise ship

There was a very interesting display in the tourist center, which showed all the equipment and food a Gold Rush prospector would be obliged to carry before being allowed into the Yukon by Canada's North-West Mounted Police. The NWMP established a level of law and order in the Klondike, and were stationed on the borders at the top of the passes to ensure the prospectors entering Canada had enough supplies to survive in the harsh conditions of the Klondike. The prospectors were required to carry, pull, or drag one ton of food and equipment. It is estimated that a single man carrying all that equipment in relays over the Chilkoot Pass would have to walk an incredible 2640 miles! It is unlikely that all the prospectors actually carried that much equipment and it would seem that many of them actually jettisoned some of their less useful items on the way up. We had seen some of that equipment beside the tracks as we rode the train down the mountain. In view of this, it was more likely that these men only walked a mere 1600 miles up and down the mountain to get into the Yukon to search for gold. Inevitably, many prospectors gave up and went back to wherever they came from, others became sick or were injured, while some died as a result of the terrain and the weather.

We were only in Skagway for two hours before catching the bus back to Whitehorse, and fully half that time was spent eating some not-bad fish and chips. The return journey took us up the other side of the valley, so we had a good view of the train line clinging to the valley sides across from us. But, for some reason, the bus ride just didn't have the same appeal as the train.

We got back to Whitehorse at 6:15, tired and overwhelmed with all we had seen. As we thought about this experience we realized it had only taken us a day to travel from Whitehorse to Skagway and back in relative comfort. Understanding the terrain we traveled through, we could only admire the perseverance and desperation of the men who were walking into history as part of the Klondike Gold Rush.

After the excitement of the train ride, it was now our friend Mike's turn to take charge of our tourist activities. We therefore spent the following day with Mike, being shown as much as possible of Whitehorse and its surroundings. We visited the fish ladder that climbs from the Yukon River up to an artificial lake; we saw Miles Canyon where the Yukon River has cut its way into a basalt flow from a volcanic eruption some tens of millions of years ago; and we concluded with a visit to the *SS Klondike*, a reconstructed stern-wheel steamer originally owned by the White Pass and Yukon Route, which had plied between Whitehorse and Dawson City. This beautifully reconstructed example of the type has been restored to 1938-43 glory and is meticulously furnished with either historic artifacts or reproductions of that period.

Miles Canyon (above)

The SS Klondike (below)

The city of Whitehorse runs a program in LePage Park in the summer called *Arts in the Park, which* sponsors musicians to entertain during the summer months. We took advantage of this program and enjoyed our lunch listening to the *Alaska Button Box Gang*, a dozen button accordionists doing polkas and waltzes with a rhythm section consisting of a device called a polka-cello, serrated wood blocks, a brass bell and a pair of steel pans filled with shot. It was all lighthearted fun, and after the band members announced that money from the CD sales was the only way they would be able to afford to get back to Alaska, we purchased a CD to help them on their way! While the band was playing, the Argentinean Women's fast-pitch softball team was introduced. Whitehorse was hosting an International Softball tournament and the team was there to compete. It appears they didn't do too well in the tournament, but what an experience to be visiting Canada's North.

The Alaska Button Box Gang doing their thing

After lunch it was time to have a quick look at McBride Museum where Mike was giving a lecture based on his latest book, *Dalton's Gold Rush Trail*, about the cattle drive from a farm in Saskatchewan to the Klondike, via railway and steamship, then over the Chilkat Pass from Pyramid Harbour to Fort Selkirk on the Yukon River. Since beef was fetching $40.00 a pound in the Klondike goldfields at that time, it made good financial sense to do this. It is the amazing story of a long ago entrepreneur.

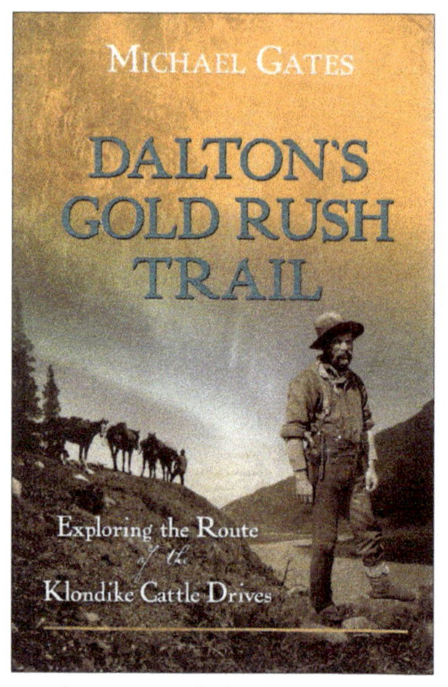

Our last evening in Whitehorse was spent in the local Mexican restaurant, *Sanchez Cantina*. The owner, Otelina Sanchez, like many other residents, was originally a visitor who came to Whitehorse for a short while and stayed. This is a story we heard repeated many times during our travels, including Mike and Kathy, who are two of those people. This visit was a wonderful break from traveling, and Mike our local guide helped us to appreciate much more of the history and culture than would have been possible on our own.

July 13th to July 14th

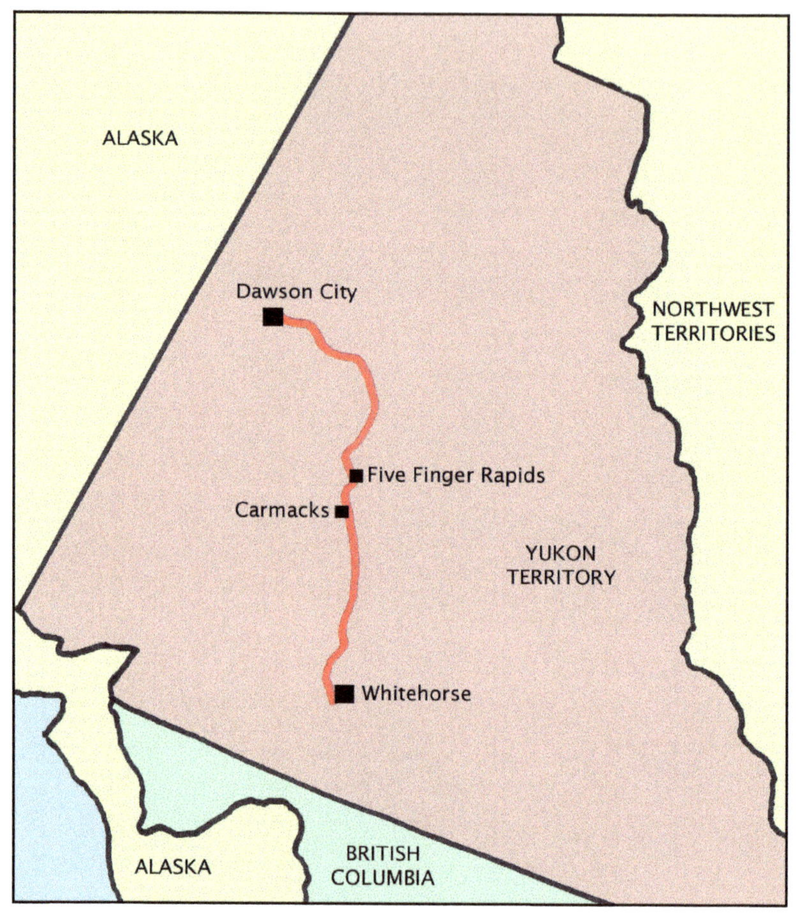

Whitehorse to Dawson City	532km
TOTAL	532km

Chapter Seven

Dawson City, Part One

We were finally on our way to Dawson City and the Dempster Highway and very thankful we didn't need to carry all our supplies on our backs. While we were in Whitehorse we learned that the Dempster had been washed out in several places and was still closed. We hoped the road would be open when we arrived in Dawson City, so we would be able to drive to Inuvik.

A Twin Lake

The great part about driving this far north was the long daylight hours, which meant that, even though we had left Whitehorse much later than we planned, it would still be light when we arrived in Dawson. It was a long day of driving with some nice interludes; buying huge cinnamon buns from the biker/owner at Braeburn Lodge with the sign 'bikers welcome'; photographing just one of the twin lakes straddling the road because the road was busy; lunch just before Carmacks at a rest stop with the most unspeakable toilets; and stopping to look over the Five Finger Rapids while chatting with a guy from North Carolina.

Five Finger Rapids, a famous hazard in the Gold Rush days

Driving into Dawson we were intrigued by the huge piles of stones and rocks on either side of the highway. We later learned they were created by the dredges that had been used to mine gold, and were now historic landmarks. However, as we passed them we wondered why they had been left in such an ugly way. But, while unappealing to look at, they are a reminder of the history of this area.

Our first stop in Dawson City was at the information centre for the

Northwest Territories, which is in the old British Yukon Navigation Building (BYN), and is the last vestige of the docks and freight buildings which once lined the waterfront. This was a good news/bad news sort of stop. The good news was that the road was open; the bad news was that the ferry to Fort McPherson across the Peel River was washed out. With no ferry, Inuvik was inaccessible by road. This was a huge disappointment but we realized this is a reality in this part of the world. After discussing our plans with the very helpful lady in the information centre we had a much better understanding of what we should and should not bring on the road. We had bought gasoline cans just in case we ran out of fuel due to scarcity of gas stations. The lady stated that the road is too rough and so cans of gas actually pose a hazard, which was some-thing we hadn't thought of. She also pointed out that Eagle Plains was less than 400 km from the start of the highway, and gas would be available there. Encouragingly, she advised us that the conditions on the Dempster can change quickly, so waiting a day in Dawson might improve the situation. We decided to spend the next day, or perhaps two, exploring Dawson City while waiting to see how things would change.

Dawson City Post Office

Dawson City was so different from anything we had seen so far. Our campsite was right in the middle of town, which meant we could walk almost everywhere. The main road is paved but the side roads are all mud and gravel, with boardwalks instead of sidewalks, and very reminiscent of the old Wild West towns seen in all those '50s and '60s westerns. As we walked about I was half expecting Wyatt Earp to ride down the street on his horse.

The buildings are typically raised from the ground to avoid subsidence due to melting permafrost

Dawson City is a Parks Canada Heritage Site and has been restored to keep the historical flavour of the Gold Rush era. We observed that the exteriors of the houses in the main part of the town had been maintained to preserve their original character. And in keeping with this, there were a number of stores selling gold mined in the Yukon, both in the form of the nuggets—unrefined gold—and as beautiful jewelry made by local goldsmiths. We also saw jewelry made from fossil mammoth ivory, which is found periodically by miners working around Dawson City. As we wandered through town we came across old houses that had been built on the permafrost many years ago, and were now falling and sinking into ground as their heating gradually melted the permafrost below; the reality of building in the North, and something to think about. We hoped to visit the Commissioner's Residence, a large and beautiful building, but when we arrived it was closed. We learned later all the various historic sites in Dawson are only opened on a rotating basis due to limited staffing. So we checked out the Museum instead. Many years ago Bob had given a workshop in this building and it brought back memories. There were many really interesting exhibits concerning life in this area through the Gold Rush and beyond, and it made us think of the differences, both social and physical, between then and now. After a happy hour spent in the museum it was back to exploring more of Dawson City.

A line of trucks waiting for the Dempster Highway to open

Dawson City had its fair share of flooding over the years, and in 1986 a dike was built to protect the town from the risk of further floods, and a park was created as part of the dike. We strolled in the park along the Yukon River and noticed a line of trucks parked along the road, doubtless waiting for the Dempster Highway to reopen after the flooding. At this point I remembered a sign I had seen the previous day advertising an outdoor market and as this was the day, I thought it would be a nice idea to check it out.

We met one vendor selling spruce syrup and specialty jams. By her accent it was clear that she wasn't from here, so inevitably we started chatting. She had come from Hampshire, England about nine years ago to travel in the North and had fallen in love with the place. So she stayed, settled here and then married. Now she and her husband live outside Dawson City without running water or electrical power. We were curious about how she tolerated the long, dark winters this far north. Her answer was simple; it's often so clear that you have the moon for almost the whole month, and the light off the pristine snow means it's never really dark. She said that this is so totally different to the grayness and dullness of the southern English winter they cannot be compared. Bob and I both agreed with that. There seemed to be a strong hint of the romantic in her story; still she is obviously very happy here. As we wandered away from her stall, we wondered if it can really be that clear and light and how we would find living here in the winter. We left her stall after buying pots of spruce syrup and some jam to use carefully, since it seemed unlikely we would be able to replace them soon.

The next stall we visited was advertising fresh vegetables. The owner claimed her market garden was the furthest north in Canada. To our surprise and delight we were able to buy good quality fresh produce all grown here in Dawson.

Fresh vegetables grown in Dawson City

We walked slowly back to the campsite where I had an interesting conversation with a lady from California—as identified by the very dirty licence plates on the car—whose children had written Dempster Highway in the mud on her station wagon. "So, I see you were on the Dempster. How was it?" was my opening question. She described the trip with her husband and two kids. They could get no further than the Peel River ferry since it was washed out when they got there, but they tent-camped there; saw a Grizzly Bear, wolves, caribou and some smaller wildlife. Quite the adventure for the family and something I am sure the children will never forget.

After supper that evening we started a conversation with our neighbours in the camper next to us. This couple were originally from north-eastern

Australia, had been living and working in New York for four years, and were visiting their son in Whitehorse. They had taken this opportunity to travel further north and spoke about their work with some passion, telling us of the challenges they faced working with the inner city children of New York. Our discussion ranged over education, healthcare, democracy and monarchy as we all enjoyed a couple of glasses of wine. The conversation finally broke up when we realized it was past midnight and still light. Not the early night we had planned since we were going to tackle the Dempster Highway in the morning.

VEGETABLES
DAWSON CITY
FARMERS MARKET
YUKON
BIRCH
Syrup

July 15th to July 17th

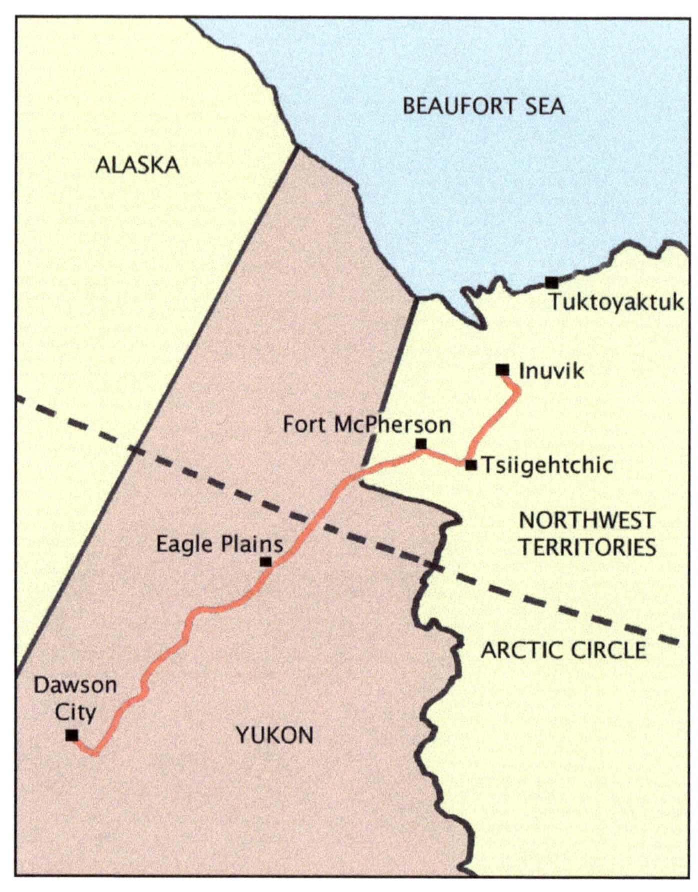

Dawson City to Eagle Plains	404km
Eagle Plains to Inuvik	399km
TOTAL	803km

Chapter Eight
The Dempster Highway North

Finally it was time to learn what the Dempster was all about. We left Dawson City knowing the Peel River ferry was washed out, but we were hopeful it would be opened the following day. If we weren't able to get to Inuvik, our back-up plan was to stay at Eagle Plains for the night, and then at least drive to the ferry—which would mean crossing the Arctic Circle and entering the Northwest Territories—then drive back to Eagle Plains for the night, returning to Dawson City the following day. While this was not an ideal plan, we thought it a viable if not satisfactory option.

The Dempster Highway is a gravel road over 700km long heading north/north-east over several mountain ranges. The engineering involved in building this road is impressive. For most of the way the road sits on permafrost and has incredible terrain to deal with; mountains, rivers, tundra and rocks, and overlying it all, extreme weather issues. From the road surface the highway looks like a huge berm many metres wide and high, which insulates the road from the permafrost. This keeps the road drivable during the summer months. In the winter it becomes an ice road and, according the truckers we met, is much easier to drive.

As we left Dawson City we found the gas station near the southern end of the Dempster Highway, and filled the vehicle up with as much gas as we could. That would get us to Eagle Plains without too much difficulty, or so we hoped. Everything inside the living portion of the RV was padded or tied down; bungee cords were everywhere, and even the microwave plate was removed from its usual place and safely placed in our bed (both the bed and plate were clean) to prevent it bouncing around and jumping out. After all our work we hoped we had everything covered, but still wondered what the road would throw at us.

Given everything we had heard about the road, we planned to alternate the driving every 100km or so, which proved to be a good decision. This is a gravel/mud/dust road, so as we drove along the van rattled and shook, our belongings jumped around, and generally the whole vehicle sounded very unhappy. But the views...! The scenery is spectacular; amazing mountains, huge rushing rivers, wonderful forests dwindling eventually to tundra. There had been a great deal of rain, which resulted in much water rushing through; swollen rivers in huge valleys, many of which passed under the road by means of culverts. We could only imagine the force of the water flooding over the road and washing it out, so the lack of bridges started to make sense: what kind of bridge would be able stand up to all that water?

Vistas like this became commonplace as the highway climbed and fell through the Ogilvie Mountains

As we started on the highway we were lulled into a false sense of security because the first 5km was paved. Then it descended into gravel and washboard. The washboard surface was absolutely terrible and the thought of two days of driving on this surface was horrifying; it would wreck us and the RV. Mercifully this didn't last for too long before we encountered hard-packed mud, which made a reasonable driving surface. Still, the back of the van became covered in wet, sticky, cloying mud, with no back window and no tail lights visible! We stopped for a bathroom break and orientation to the area in the Ogilvie Mountains at the Tombstone Park campground information centre. We got an update on the Peel River ferry (which wasn't promising) and then went on our way, onwards and upwards literally. The vegetation initially was trees, bushes, wildflowers and grasses, but this changed as we went further north.

Our mud collection after the first 80km or so

As we left Tombstone Park (named for the mountains in the area) it was raining and miserable, so when we saw a hitchhiker we naturally stopped and offered him a ride. His name was Roman and he was from the Bordeaux area of France, so we chatted about France as we drove. He was really nice guy, but had obviously been living rough for a while and hadn't had good access to laundry and shower facilities. He was happy not to be walking since he had been hitchhiking, walking and camping out for several days. We had learned early on that most people on this road are friendly, so picking up a hitchhiker didn't seem have the same risks as in the south.

As we drove further we met the potholes. Now, we had heard horror stories about tires from several sources: the 'razor-sharp' shale, the 'shredded tires' and the innumerable blow-outs, but we were comforted by the knowledge of the spares we were carrying. We were equipped with a six-ton hydraulic jack and knew how to use it if need be, so while we were concerned about punctures we felt we could cope. However, on this never-to-be-forgotten excursion punctures were not the concern. We met potholes! Most drivers in Canada are used to potholes in the winter, and more often in the spring. Well forget them; they don't match up to anything on the Dempster. These potholes were in patterns up and down the road, and were filled with mud. Some of them were in straight lines where the vehicles had traveled, so there was lots of swerving and driving on the wrong side of the road, the middle of the road, over to the edge (you get the picture) just to avoid the worst of them. Then there were potholes that had multiplied and become mummy and daddy potholes with lots of baby potholes all over the road. And once they were settled into nice family groupings, they had invited grandpa and grandma potholes to join them! Then, when the road felt you needed more challenge it developed muddy ruts around the potholes so the mud would grip the wheels and take them places you didn't want them to go. This surface was the one we faced most of the way to Eagle Plains, about 375km in all.

The Ogilvie Mountains with the rain mercifully letting up

All this was going on while the road wound and twisted its way around rocks, lakes, rivers and mountains, going up and down, and at one point reaching over 1400m above sea level. And just when you think you can't go on any longer, a piece of nice flat hard-packed road with no potholes appears and fools you into thinking it's going to continue this way. It doesn't! These short flat stretches are likely the best maintained pieces of the highway because they also double as landing strips for light aircraft. It is odd to drive along a road with a couple of wind socks on the side and signs telling you not to stop because this is a landing strip.

We were alternating driving, which allowed both of us to enjoy the ride, because the driver could only focus on the road and perhaps the wild-flowers and bushes at the edges of the road. The passenger, on the other hand, can look around and enjoy the most breath-taking vistas; long views towards mountains kilometres distant with the road winding its way through them; valleys with mountains either side of them and a river or brook rushing through; fields of wildflowers. And on the plateaus the mountain ranges, valleys and rivers spread out on both sides of the road. All totally stunning.

Here you can see how the road surface is raised on a gravel berm above the permafrost

At one point we stopped for lunch near one of the many streams along the way. As I made lunch Bob and Roman went for a brief walk, but soon returned to the vehicle because the swarms of mosquitoes were also hungry and trying to use the two guys as their lunch counter. We drove through a deep, wide glaciated valley with many little lakes and streams, and hosts of wildflowers, but less in the way of wildlife; a couple of gophers and rabbits, and the occasional grouse-like bird, possibly ptarmigan, were all we saw. The road found its way up to a plateau via Seven Mile Hill, and as I was driving this piece I can affirm that it really felt that long. The road had really deteriorated by this time and I was maxing out at 40kph! And me with the lead foot! It was rough, with potholes, rocks and mud; the vehicle slipped and slid all over the road at the whim of the mud. It felt a bit like driving in snow, but even more slippery. Finally I reached the top and then it was more of the same all along the plateau which seemed to go on forever. We stopped a few times to admire the views and at one stop met a Swiss cyclist who was riding to Inuvik with another person. He and our hitchhiker were happy to chat to each other, while we discussed with awe the determination shown in cycling this kind of road. The scenery continued to amaze us, and was continually changing; the trees were becoming smaller and sparser with every kilometre we drove. It was a landscape like none I had ever seen before.

On the high plains approaching Eagle Plains one has a panoramic view of the Ogilvie River winding through its valley

As we were nearing Eagle Plains we approached a car that had skidded off the road and was sitting at an angle beside the highway. As this road is not that well traveled we stopped and investigated. Fortunately, no one was in the car but all their belongings were still there. We reported the incident when we got to Eagle Plains and were told that they knew about it, and that the car had been there for some time. There seems to be an unwritten code of conduct up here; there is a lot of road and not many people, so if you see a car off to the side, or if someone seems to be in trouble, you stop and check it out since you may be the only person around for a long time.

We finally arrived at Eagle Plains at around 4:30pm, having left Dawson City at about 8:00am, and signed in to the campsite for the night. We created some amusement for our neighbours parked on each side. The back-up camera was totally covered in mud, as was the rest of the vehicle, so Bob had to reverse into our designated spot while I stood outside in the mud gesticulating wildly to make sure we didn't bump either of the neighbouring RVs. The owners watching the two of us were provided with free entertainment for the night.

The hotel at Eagle Plains

Although we were aware of the ferry closure, we had no idea of what this really meant to the traffic on the highway. At Eagle Plains we realized the impact of this particular road closure: the parking lot and lodge were filled with over 50 trucks and truckers who were stuck here because they couldn't get to Inuvik until the Peel River ferry was back in service. Some of the trucks were on the regular route and others were carrying military supplies for a big exercise that summer. We learned that many of the trucks had been there for four to five days, and to the best of everyone's knowledge the ferry wouldn't be running for a couple more days. Since many of the trucks were carrying perishables this was really and issue for both them and the population to the north of the Peel River.

Trucks waiting at Eagle Plains until the ferry reopened

We spoke to the drivers, since they were the most experienced and well informed users of this road, to get their feeling about the ferry and hence the road opening up soon. While they were hopeful, they had several reservations. The general feeling was once the ferry was open the trucks would go first, especially those carrying food and gas. The big concern was the water level; if it was still very high, the ferry would only take one truck on each run, and with the soft ramps being built it was likely there would be problems with loading and unloading. We heard that some truck drivers carrying perishables had driven up to the Peel River to see if they could ship their cargos across by boat, to be loaded onto empty trucks on the other side, and thus driven to Inuvik. We didn't hear if this strategy worked, but it made us both realize how far away we were from our comfortable home in Ottawa. Our biggest complaint might be about the cost of those perishable items, rather than actual access to them due to poor road conditions.

After these discussions we decided to revert to our alternative plan of driving to the Arctic Circle marker, taking some pictures and coming back to figure out new plans for the unexpected extra time, since staying at Eagle Plains indefinitely was not an option. We were disappointed, but we had no control over the weather and the condition of the road, so we had to make the best of it. While we were pondering our options, we met a couple from San Diego who were heading up to Inuvik in their pickup truck/camper van, complete with their old blind and deaf cat. So we chatted and compared notes about the route so far, little realizing how important this encounter was to be.

We had supper in the RV as we listened to the rain come down! We really didn't need more rain; it would only make the road muddier still, and it wouldn't even clean the existing mud off the vehicle. After supper the rain had stopped and we took advantage of the break, went over to the restaurant and bar and called our daughter and her family on the public phone in the lobby. We were learning that the cell and WiFi coverage up north is not the same as in the south, so a public pay phone was a boon. Then the rain started up again, which gave us the excuse to have tea and coffee in the restaurant, along with the many other people stranded here. We chatted to a very nice woman from Montreal who had been traveling on her own all over Mexico, the States and Canada for over a year. She had given up her apartment, sold, given away or stored all her possessions and taken to the road in her little Pleasureway, a large and well-equipped van ideal for one person. Her stories of places she had seen, and descriptions of places we should visit made for a very pleasant way to spend a rainy evening.

The Arctic Circle at latitude 66° 33' north (although our GPS didn't agree by quite a margin)

Roman, our hitchhiker from Bordeaux, poses for his portrait at the Arctic Circle marker

It was no longer raining when we woke in the morning, so we planned to drive up to Peel River to see how our future looked regarding getting to Inuvik. After collecting our hitchhiker, who had done laundry and had a shower, we drove off to the Arctic Circle, about 40km from Eagle Plains. After the requisite photos with the Arctic Circle marker we decided to drive a bit further and see how far we could get, maybe to the border of the Northwest Territories and perhaps to the Peel River. However, we were feeling somewhat discouraged, so after our lunch break we started the journey back to Eagle Plains and a return to Dawson City. It was a sad moment, but at that time it seemed to make sense.

We dropped our hitchhiker off at Engineer's Creek campground, one of several along the Dempster, and after wishing him well we continued towards Eagle Plains. A few kilometres down the road we spotted the couple from San Diego coming towards as and waving furiously, so we pulled over wondering if they had some kind of problem. No, not a problem, but good news: the ferry at Peel River was open! So we turned around again and headed back north, our poor RV getting quite dizzy with all the changes in our plans.

Things were definitely looking up. As we headed north again we wondered what our ex-hitchhiker was doing, and if he had heard the good news. Should we pick him up again if we saw him? Naturally, when we saw him beside the road with his thumb out we picked him up again, and made those tongue in cheek introductions all over again. We were all laughing by the end of it. Now it was time to head for the ferry at the Peel River.

The road to the ferry passes through the most gorgeous scenery. We were driving on the high plains with views over the rivers below and the Richardson Mountain range to the east. The road skirts the mountains for the longest while, then takes the plunge and decides to go through them. The Wright Pass took us over the top and into the Northwest Territories, where we stopped to take pictures and chat to our friends from San Diego.

The border of the Northwest Territories at the top of the pass

A pause at the border and a chat with the friends who had stopped us and told us about the ferry

The Mackenzie Delta extending to the horizon

After passing the Northwest Territories border marker it's a long downhill stretch until suddenly you come to the edge of the plain and there before you is the Mackenzie Delta spread out to the horizon. It is absolutely stunning and our pictures simply can't capture it.

We finally arrived at the ferry line-up and joined it about one kilometre from the front. Our friends who had stopped to tell us about the ferry were right behind us, so we all walked down to see what was happening with the ramps. This was about 3:00 or 4:00pm, and the rumour mill was in full swing with the general thought was it would take until about 9:00pm to get the earthen ramps rebuilt. Once operating, the ferry would run until all the vehicles were over. This led to the discussion of how we could manage this: who sleeps, who stays awake, when do we eat, and so on? The cable ferry over the Peel River normally takes about five minutes to load, five minutes to cross the river and five minutes to unload and then follows the same cycle on the return trip. When we walked down to the ramp all we saw were the guys working at building up the earth ramps. We watched as a front-end loader brought gravel from a storage pile while a bulldozer leveled the ramp, so now we understood why it might take until 9:00 to actually start ferrying the cars and trucks. I was a little surprised as I looked at the gradually growing ramp, because in my ignorance I thought the ramps would be like those I was used to in Ontario, with lots of concrete and properly paved!! To see plain gravel ramps was a bit of a shock, but really, what else could they do when working with huge rivers, spring floods and permafrost?

We wait in line while a backhoe and bulldozer rebuild the ramps

We were slowly ambling back to the vehicle when a young kid raced up to tell his family that the ferry would start to load soon, beginning with the cars and RVs. Everyone with a car or RV rapidly returned to their vehicles, pulled out of the line and created a second line-up. We still weren't sure it would happen, but we were all ready for the ferry if it actually ran. Because the trucks had been so delayed we thought initially that those carrying food would go on first, so we were very happy when the cars and RVs were allowed on. We were in the third load across the river, and that's when we realized why they put the lightest vehicles through first. The newly-built ramps were very soft and the cars and RVs were sinking in horribly. Bob was concerned we would be stuck, but then the loading guy yelled, “Give ’er!”, so he stamped down and we rumbled and skidded up the ramp to where we needed to be. We later heard that due to the soft ramps each truck had to be winched on and off the ferry because they were sinking so badly into the soft gravel.

It was now almost 7:30 and still completely light. We wanted to make it into Inuvik that night, so when we arrived at the second ferry, which crossed the Mackenzie at Tsiigehtchic, I made a snack for the road. We met our new best friends again, and chatted to them while we waited. Finally, we actually exchanged names! Sandy and Brett were across first, and we followed on the next crossing. As we drove away from the Mackenzie River we came across hundreds of rabbits jumping all over the road, and were quite surprised at the sight. We were also much happier with the road at this point. Finally, the surface was much harder and drier, and although there were a number of potholes, overall the conditions were much better than our experiences of the previous day.

We arrived in Inuvik at around 11:45pm and found the nearest campsite, happily in the centre of town. It was still bright and sunny with a few clouds, and by the time we were settled in to our camp spot it was Bob’s birthday so we celebrated both it and our arrival in Inuvik with a glass of wine. Right from the start of this adventure Bob had said he wanted to celebrate his birthday in Inuvik under the midnight sun, and even with all the trials and tribulations of the last couple of days, we had fulfilled his dream.

The midnight sun greets us at our campsite in Inuvik

July 17th to July 21st

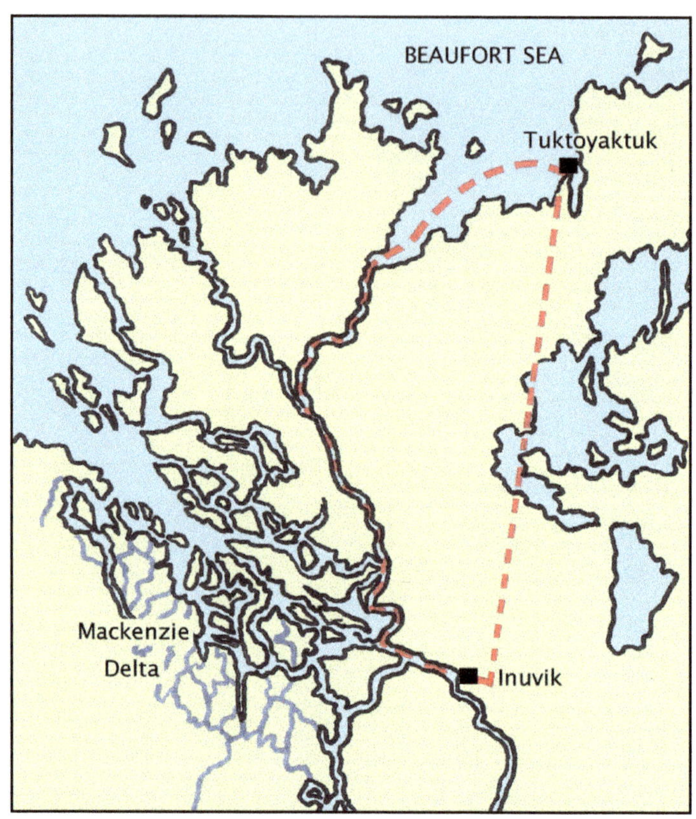

Inuvik to Tuktoyaktuk (boat)	6 hours
Tuktoyaktuk to Inuvik (plane)	30 minutes

Chapter Nine
Inuvik and Tuktoyaktuk

After our late arrival and celebration the previous evening we spent some time over breakfast, reflecting on those early dreams of coming here in our new RV. While we always believed we could do this, we did question whether we *would* actually do it. And here we were in Inuvik on Bob's birthday, the pinnacle of our hopes and dreams.

The first task was to find the tour company for our trip to Tuktoyaktuk. After all, we had come so far that we couldn't miss seeing the Arctic Ocean. We found the Up North Tours booking agent in the lobby of one of the local hotels, made a booking for July 19th, and learned that the trip would start at 6:00am at the Up North Tours office. The tour guide would be taking us by boat to Tuktoyaktuk, and after a tour there we would be dropped off at the airport and fly back to Inuvik, where we would be met on our return. We were pleased to learn that Up North Tours is an entirely aboriginal-owned company.

The booking done it was time to go shopping. Bob had requested beef bourguignon for his birthday dinner, so our next stop was the grocery store where we were pleasantly surprised at the prices. After picking up the needed items we set off to the Western Arctic Regional Visitor Centre where we received the official documents certifying our arrival above the Arctic Circle.

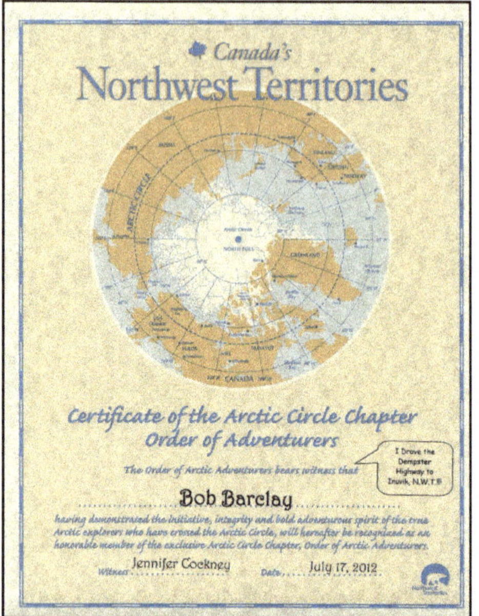

Canada's
Northwest Territories

Certificate of the Arctic Circle Chapter
Order of Adventurers

The Order of Arctic Adventurers bears witness that

I Drove the Dempster Highway to Inuvik, N.W.T.!!

Bob Barclay

having demonstrated the initiative, integrity and bold adventurous spirit of the true Arctic explorers who have crossed the Arctic Circle, will hereafter be recognized as an honorable member of the exclusive Arctic Circle Chapter, Order of Arctic Adventurers.

Witness: Jennifer Cockney Date: July 17, 2012

Our certification as visitors to the Northwest Territories

The Western Arctic Regional Visitor Centre with a sculpture in the foreground

The famous Igloo Church was the next stop, and after that we just wandered around the town noticing how different things were here. For example, we were fascinated by all the exterior plumbing. Because of the permafrost, all the conduits bringing water and electricity to the houses and removing waste water were insulated and above ground. This, together with raising the houses on mini stilts, is a practical way of coping with the permafrost.

The Igloo Church (left)

Above-ground plumbing and houses on stilts (below)

Our campground was the only one in the centre of Inuvik, so we were happy to meet Sandy and Brett when they arrived. They had stopped earlier than us the night before, and had stayed in a campground a little way outside Inuvik. Other campers happily told us about the air show the military were putting on that evening, just for Bob's birthday apparently! The campground actually overlooked the airfield, which meant we had prime seats for the show.

Another couple were towing a very fancy rowboat, and told us about their son and his three friends who were about to row across the Arctic Ocean to Russia. These four guys were extreme adventurers; rowing across the Atlantic, climbing Everest, swimming across the English

Channel, etc. We took a good look at the boat, which was equipped with all the most up to date mod-cons including solar panels, wind generator, sat phones, a GPS that sent their location automatically every 15 seconds, and so on. The team left Inuvik on July 17th and arrived at Port Hope, Alaska 41 days later having rowed over 1,000 miles. They were short of their goal, but given the terrible weather they encountered, it was a phenomenal achievement.

The rowboat for a trip to Russia

Back at the campsite we encountered a figure we recognized. During our drive up to Inuvik, we had come across several cyclists. Given the conditions, they were either splattered unrecognizably with mud or vanishing into clouds of dust. We had noticed this guy while waiting at the Peel River ferry. He had panniers either side of his front wheel, matching panniers at the rear, a rack across the back, and the frame festooned with bottles and bags. At that time we commented on the dedication of cycling this road. Two days later there he was at our campsite in Inuvik. He told us he had pedaled from Tacoma, Washington and didn't make much of a big deal of it, saying he had the time to travel slowly, which allowed for his perceived lack of stamina. He just thought if you're in no particular hurry to get anywhere you can take your time, which he did. Just the thought of contemplating those distances was simply exhausting, and we admired his dedication in riding all this way. After all, he had to face the ride back, all 730km of it.

Roman, our erstwhile hitchhiker, had found a tenting spot in our campground where he met a number of other hitchhikers, cyclists and young people traveling light. It was interesting to note that the 'tenters' didn't sleep on the ground, but had raised wooden platforms with anchors for guy ropes, yet another accommodation for the permafrost.

Suddenly we were back in the social whirl. After Bob's birthday dinner we watched the air show while chatting to a number of campers. The air show itself was really good; mainly military aircraft: helicopters, fighter jets, an Aurora search and rescue plane, and a Twin Otter. There were parachute jumpers and the show naturally finished off with the Snowbirds. After the show Roman invited us out for a drink to thank us for driving him up here. So, once the Snowbirds had flown away, we went off with him to the Hotel Mackenzie, one of the better bars in town. We were soon joined by a couple of young women, who were also hitchhiking their way around the North and had already met Roman, so we chatted with them for a while as well. On our walk back to the RV that night we realized we were already adapting to the long days and staying up much later than we would do at home.

We had arrived in Inuvik at the perfect time. The Great Northern Arts Festival, an annual celebration, was in full swing, giving the priceless opportunity to enjoy the work of artisans and performers from around the Arctic Circle. We had no idea we would be here for this wonderful occasion. The following morning we and our friends wandered over to the Community Centre where the craft market was set up. There were some wonderful crafts; beading, woven pieces, carvings and so on. Some of the artisans, whose work was on display and for sale, were working in the centre of the room, so the casual visitor could actually see how the various crafts were done. I found a wonderful yarn called *qiviut*, which is made from the under-down of the muskox and is incredibly warm and soft. I spent some time with the artisan who had spun and dyed the yarn, and we talked about the yarn and its uses. While we were talking she showed me how she picked the under-down off the muskox skin, slow and tedious work but well worth it in my view. The yarn itself was very expensive but having seen the work involved in harvesting it, I understand why. I loved the yarn but I wasn't sure about buying it, until Bob said, "It's less than the price of a tank of gas!" Back at home, I knitted it into a lovely lacy, very warm scarf which is invaluable for winter use. I really believe it is one of the warmest things I own, and it is feather light.

The skein of qiviut knitted into a scarf

After spending some time at the craft market, the four of us went to meet a German youth counselor who was working with the young people in Inuvik. He was another one of those who had come up to the North, had fallen in love with the country and had stayed to work here. He was also very well informed about the issues facing the youth in this community, and enthusiastic about the programs the Youth Centre offered.

Dancing, drumming and singing at the Great Northern Arts Festival

In the evening there was a performance of Inuit drumming and dancing. This was a very different and interesting experience from the dancing and drumming we had seen on the West Coast and in Ontario. The dances represented important stories or occasions, and a commentary was given about each one. After the more formal dances the audience were invited to join in, and were encouraged by the dancers to do so. There were lots of military personnel at the show, and several of them went onto the floor, much to the delight of the audience. Bob also jumped up and took part in a couple of the dances. We left before the dancing was over because the early start for the trip to Tuk precluded a second late night.

It was still bright when we walked back to the campground. It was very different being this far north and having continuous daylight, and it changed the way we thought and acted. Young children were still up and playing at 10:30pm and nobody seemed to mind. Judging by our own reaction to the very long days, it was understandable why so many people, children in particular, were still up very late at night. Who wants to sleep when the sun is shining, especially as in six months the sun will not be visible at all?

The following day we would go as far north as we could on this trip; to Tuktoyaktuk. After a very early start we and our fellow travelers were taken to the river dock by our Inuit guide, Gerry. We climbed into a small boat with a closed front cabin and a large outboard motor. Gerry introduced himself and told us a little about the cruise we were embarking on, a trip down the East Channel of the Mackenzie, which would include a couple of stops, arriving in Tuk by early afternoon. We would then be met by a second guide who would show us around Tuk, and finally take us to the airport for the short flight back to Inuvik. Gerry's cousin and family had traveled here all the way from Yellowknife by boat and would follow us to Tuktoyaktuk. Seeing this family and understanding how far they had traveled gave us more appreciation of the vastness of the North and the various ways people use to travel through this huge land.

The trip to Tuk took about six hours and was punctuated by a couple of stops. The first stop was at the sand hills. In the winter big trucks and front-end loaders travel the ice road to collect sand and gravel, all naturally occurring, and bring it back to Inuvik for use throughout the year. Gerry talked about the ice road that goes to Tuktoyaktuk and cuts the travel time to and from Inuvik significantly. Several of the group climbed up the sand hills and met the mosquitoes of this area. They were extremely persistent and the only escape was the wind generated by the motion of the boat as we traveled the Mackenzie.

As we continued down the river we encountered endless vistas of eroded river banks and stunted trees. And the sky was not to be outdone, with its many variations of cloud, rainbow and rain shadow. Together, the colours of the vegetation and sky were quite delightful. As we went further we noticed the tree line dipping down a little, probably due to the comparative warmth of the river but then, as the boat continued towards the mouth of the delta, the trees faded back and the scenery become more typically tundra.

The eroded banks of the Mackenzie

Our second stop was at a hunt camp where we met Clara and her family. Clara had prepared a meal for us, laid out on a table in a mesh dining tent in an attempt to reduce our exposure to the local mosquitoes. The meal was really interesting, consisting of fried caribou, mashed potatoes and bannock, with side dishes of whale meat, muktuk (whale blubber) and three kinds of smoked fish. We had tea to accompany the meal. The caribou was delicious as was the bannock, which had been cooked on a griddle, giving it a really good flavour. Bob enjoyed the smoked fish, and we all tried the whale offerings. These were greeted with a variety of comments from our fellow travelers, both negative and positive, while our guide Gerry commented that for him blue cheese and sauerkraut were hard to eat! It is all about enjoying the food you know.

Glorious cloud formations and effects of lighting seen from the boat

Gerry told us about hunting caribou and whale. For his extended family one whale will supply all their needs for a year. The whale is cut up, dried and smoked, and then stored away. Stan, Clara's son, showed us his smokehouse where he hangs up filleted fish (mostly whitefish but sometimes herring) and smokes them with driftwood for two or three days. He also showed us his whale hunting gear. Much to our surprise it looked exactly the same as the museum pieces we have seen, but using more modern materials. This whole experience reminded us that there are still people who depend on the land and sea for sustenance, something that is frequently forgotten when the local store is only a short drive away.

Whale harpoon and gaff (above)

Clara describes the food she has prepared (left)

The tundra consists of low bushes, shrubs, flowers, mosses and lichens, and is spongy to walk upon, as the group discovered as they crossed it to view a large pingo a little way behind the hunt camp. I had never heard of pingos before and was fascinated to learn about them. They are formed when a lake situated over permafrost dries up; the pressure of freezing in the winter forces an ice core upwards and this is repeated year after year, so a cone of soil rises, with a solid ice core at the top. Tuktoyaktuk has Canada's largest and oldest pingo, which rivals others found in Russia.

These pingos are the largest in Canada

While the rest of the group took a walk on the tundra, I took this wonderful opportunity to talk to Clara and learn something of her life. Her family have been coming to this location for many years, arriving at the start of the ice break-up and ending with the last of the wild berries. She loves the camp and spends as much time as she can out there. Because of her love for the outdoors, Clara sold her city house to her daughter and chose to spend most of her time in the bush rather than in city. She spoke about teaching her daughters to hunt whale and caribou, which all four daughters have done very successfully. When I spoke to her daughter she talked about her love for the camp, which she and her children visit during the hunting season; being able to relax and enjoy the quietness. Just sitting in the hunt camp the silence was noticeable. Other than the sounds of the group on the tundra, the silence around us was profound, and as there was no wind on the day we were visiting there was nothing to disturb the peace. It was quite beautiful and to us city dwellers most unusual.

The smokehouse (above) and the house at the hunt camp (left)

I was invited into Clara's home and she politely asked me to remove my shoes when I came in. It was a small room with beds and cots all along one wall, a kitchen area in corner and an eating-type area in another. I wished I had more time to talk to Clara and her daughter and learn more about their life, but it was time to return to the boat. Just before I left, I checked out the family bathroom, otherwise known as the outhouse. Its door faced away from the house and it was nicely appointed with good toilet paper and a proper seat. The door was a piece of wood at the bottom and a curtain the rest of the way. And while it may have seemed somewhat primitive, it was better than many outhouses I have seen and used in provincial parks and other places!

After six hours traveling down the delta we were in the Beaufort Sea and close to Tuktoyaktuk. It was only while I was sailing on the river that I actually realized just how big it was. The river itself is huge, and the delta is vast. As Gerry told us, the only other river delta in North America bigger than the Mackenzie is the Mississippi. This was a surprise, but having traveled one part of the delta, I can believe it.

The approach to Tuktoyaktuk from the Beaufort Sea

Our visit to Tuktoyaktuk was quite informal. Our guide wasn't there to meet us, so we said goodbye to Gerry and wandered around the dock area. We noticed a couple of sod houses in not very good condition, and later learned that in a place with little wood or building materials, a house warm enough for the winter could be built using driftwood with a sod covering. A very different way of coping with the frigid temperatures of the Northern winter. Once John, our guide, arrived in a small bus the tour began. Our first stop was the icehouse. This was an innocuous sounding name, creating visions of a shed with lots of straw and lumps of ice, but like so much of what we saw it was not so simple here in the North. From the outside the icehouse looked like a small outhouse painted white, but inside was a long ladder leading down several metres into the permafrost. Passageways and rooms had been carved out of the permafrost and used as frozen storage for the residents of the area, a very practical way of using the environment to preserve food.

The icehouse above ground and deep in the permafrost

Then we visited the Anglican Church, complete with pump organ, which was a sturdily built log house heated with a stove. In keeping with everything else, materials locally available were used. For example, some of the wall hangings were made of decorated sealskin depicting religious themes. The organ, made by D.W. Karn of Woodstock, Ontario in the early 20th century, is used on a regular basis. I wondered what the journey had been like for this pretty organ, and just how long it took to find its way to such a remote place as Tuk. We really enjoyed seeing this lovely little building which was so much in tune with its environment.

Interior of the Anglican church showing the sealskin altar decoration

A little reed organ by Karn of Woodstock, Ontario. One hundred years and still in use

As we drove away from the church we saw the little ship that had brought the first Catholic missionaries to Tuk. It is raised on blocks on dry land, and it made one wonder how they made it so far north in such a small vessel.

The little vessel that brought missionaries to Tuktoyaktuk

The houses in Tuk, like the ones in Inuvik, are all supported on short pillars to keep them off the permafrost, but unlike in Inuvik they have no conduits for water or sewage. Instead, each house has storage tanks for sewage and water, and the appropriate trucks come round every one to two days to pump water in and remove the sewage. The tanks hold around 400 gallons, although some larger families have bigger ones. Living here in the North certainly has challenges that I had not thought about.

When we first planned this trip and discussed going to Tuktoyaktuk, I had wished to see the Trans Canada Trail marker. We have been supporters of the Trail for many years and our son Ian had used the trail on his many cycle trips, both to the East and to the West. There are three important markers for the Trans Canada Trail; Tuktoyaktuk NWT, Tofino BC and St John's NFL, which mark the beginning and end of the trail from sea to sea to sea. Ian had seen the markers in Tofino and St Johns, and now it was our turn to see the third one in Tuktoyaktuk, an exciting experience for us.

The Trans Canada Trail marker

As we had come this far north we felt an obligation to at least wade in the Arctic Ocean. So John took us to a little beach to do just that. When we arrived there was a mass of driftwood which had come in a couple of days earlier, which made for an interesting walk to the edge of the water. Then the whole tour group courageously waded into the ocean. To our surprise, the water was not that cold and it actually felt good on the feet, so we stayed there for a few minutes.

When we received certificates commemorating this experience we were amused at the various options offered, including skinny dipping in the Arctic! We asked our guide if anyone had checked that option off, and he said that a few people had actually done that.

ARCTIC OCEAN TOE DIPPING
CERTIFICATE
This is to certify that
JANET BARCLAY
Having demonstrated courage and bravery by:
☒ Toe Dipping ☐ Wading
☐ Swimming ☐ Skinny Dipping
In the icy cold waters of the Arctic Ocean at Tuktoyaktuk, Northwest Territories
and is now an Honourable Member of the
EXCLUSIVE ARCTIC OCEAN TOE DIPPING ADVENTURERS CLUB OF THE WESTERN ARCTIC
JULY 19 2012
Date
Witness

Dipping our feet in the Arctic Ocean, skipping a few stones and getting a certificate for it

The next stop on the tour was a pingo and a short climb to the top. Bob climbed the pingo with the rest of the group while I watched. He had a good view of the town from the top, and could see a nascent pingo in a nearby lake. According to John, it had not been there when he was young, and over the last few years he has seen it slowly grow.

A view of Tuktoyaktuk from the top of the pingo

It was now the end of a long day and time to leave Tuktoyaktuk and fly back to Inuvik, but first we stopped off on the way to the airport to take a picture of the town sign. The airport was very basic: the pilot was also the check-in person, security guard and baggage handler. A little different from most other airports we have come though in the last few years. Our plane was a six-seat Cessna, and the flight was surprisingly smooth. As we flew over the tundra we could look down on hundreds and hundreds of small lakes. In Ontario the lakes would all have names, but here the whole landscape is mutable; these lakes will form and reform as the winter/summer cycle progresses. In some places we could see crack patterns in very regular geometric forms, almost as if it had been planned. The vastness of this land once more impressed itself upon us.

Our plane back to Inuvik (above)

The town sign (left)

The tundra and delta from the air

Our flight only took about 30 minutes, which was quite the contrast with the six hours we had spent on the boat. This was a wonderful experience and we were both very glad we had had the opportunity to see Tuktoyaktuk in such a rewarding manner.

After our wonderful day in Tuktoyaktuk we had one more day in Inuvik.

Because we were planning to leave the next day we thought it would be a good idea to get the RV cleaned. After all, it was wearing the Dempster Highway and it really didn't suit it. We chipped about 40 pounds of mud off all those spots we could see and reach. As we chipped away we noticed the mud was stratified, so we were able to see the various types of mud and gravel the highway workers had used in surfacing the road at various locations. It was a miniature geological map of the highway.

Dempster Highway geology laid down in mud

Then it was off to the truck wash station. This consisted of a pad of concrete for the vehicles to sit on and a long wand on a hose for washing them. While this was not the cheapest wash we had done, and not the best, the vehicle looked a lot better. We did wonder how many more layers of mud we would collect on our way back to Dawson, but felt that carrying all this extra mud was not a good idea. At the time we thought we had done a reasonable job of removing most of the mud, but several months later as we were driving the RV on good roads it developed an intermittent shimmy. This meant a quick visit to the service garage where the technicians removed another 40 pounds or so of mud from the underside! The last kick of the Dempster Highway.

Next stop was the local gas station just to make sure we would have enough fuel to get back to Eagle Plains. Bob chatted to the gas jockey, who was happy to talk about his life. He told us his favourite time of year is when he goes to the camp 'way out on the edge of the delta' to hunt for whale and caribou. He had a map of the delta pinned up in the office and showed us where the camp was. According to him, it takes four hours to get there by boat, and at times he and his friends go further afield to the west side of the delta and across the border into the Yukon where the caribou are more plentiful. Pumping gas is just a job, but seeing his eyes light up when he talked about his life out on the land emphasized the importance of the traditional way of living to the people here in the North. It was clear to us he would never move south; this is where he belongs.

On our last evening we went with Sandy and Brett to the old-time dance and fiddling competition at the community centre. The band consisted of two guitars and a fiddle. The evening started slowly; it seems that these competitions usually get going late, but by 9:15 people were up and dancing, and dancing very well. Moccasins were the dancing shoes of choice, and to us southerners it seemed odd because it was clear these beautifully beaded ones were normally worn for these occasions. In the south moccasins of such quality would be cared for and very rarely, if ever, worn. How differently we look at such things.

Once the competitive portion of the evening started, the dancers were divided into two groups; under 16 and adult. The opening dance was a full eight-pair dance with all ages participating, which looked like a lot of fun, and it was obvious that there were some gifted dancers in the group. Then the actual competition began, and we saw some really excellent dancing. The audience was fully involved, cheering on the dancers. It was clear this was a much loved and enjoyed community event. Finally, after both age groups had performed, came the results.

The band for the dance competition

A pair takes to the floor with applause from the audience

There was one young boy who had been dancing from the start. He took part in the first long jig, and then in the competition. When the results were called he was sitting on the floor with his fingers crossed. When he and his partner were called for first place, he jumped up and ran to receive his prize. It was obviously a big day for him; he was very happy and excited to win his category. To close the formal portion of the competition the winners gave the audience an encore performance.

A wonderful pair of young dancers

It was late, and as we were hoping to leave early the next morning, we headed for our campsite. As we walked back we could still hear the music, and it was clear that the dancing would go on for a long time that night. But for us, after four wonderful days in Inuvik, we would be off to other adventures.

July 21st to July 24th

Inuvik to Eagle Plains	367km
Eagle Plains to Campsite	408km
TOTAL	775km

Note: On our journey up we added extra distance by driving to the Arctic Circle marker and then back towards Eagle Plains before turning round.

Chapter Ten
The Dempster South, Dawson Again

As we headed south on the Dempster from Inuvik we wondered what the road would bring this time around. We thought it might be a more interesting drive if we took it easy and perhaps stayed overnight in Fort McPherson, one of the few towns on the highway. The road much easier going back down; the first few kilometres out of Inuvik were asphalt and then it was back to gravel again. We were reminded again of how good this part of the road actually was; a much better surface and fewer potholes. Because we had come into Inuvik late at night we had been too tired to appreciate this, so now our focus was more on the scenery, and we were better able to appreciate all the pretty little lakes and ponds seen amongst the vegetation. Driving over one creek we saw it was named 'Rabbit Creek'; remembering all the rabbits and hares we had seen on our way up, this made so much sense. This time, no doubt because it was during the day, only one rabbit was seen rushing into the undergrowth.

In what seemed like a very short time we came to the Mackenzie River ferry and crossed over, accompanied by a big rig and a pickup truck. We had been warned about the speed of the trucks, so when we drove off the ferry we pulled over and let the truck pass us, a little courtesy and much appreciated by the truckers. This drive back down the Dempster was a different experience. We were well rested, and because the road was better the driving was easier, so both the driver and passenger could look around at the spectacular vistas.

We arrived in Fort McPherson at lunchtime, much earlier than we expected, and visited the Canvas and Tent Factory. We had heard about this facility and thought it would be an interesting place to visit. It was Saturday and the production line was not running, but we were able to look around and see the kind of things produced by this remote operation. I eventually bought a little bag, which has become a favorite for 'touristing' because, though small and light, it had great capacity. A camera, water bottle, wallet, snacks all seem to fit quite easily into that little purse. While we were looking around the factory we spoke to the young woman working there and told her of our experiences in Inuvik. She lived in Fort McPherson and went to school in Inuvik, and when we told her about eating caribou and whale meat, she offered us some dried caribou her mother had given her for lunch. It had the texture of beef jerky and was somewhat fatty, but very tasty.

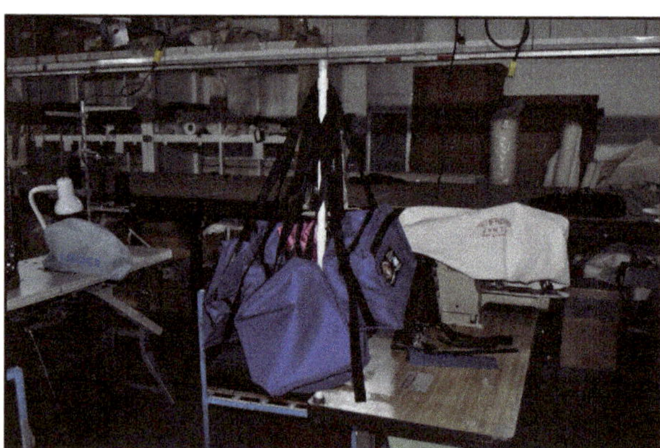

Merchandise and machinery in the Canvas and Tent Factory

While in Fort McPherson we couldn't miss a visit to the gravesite of the Lost Patrol in the Anglican cemetery. The North-West Mounted Police would travel regularly by dogsled from Dawson City to Fort McPherson and back to deliver mail and dispatches. In 1910 the team left Fort McPherson, led by Inspector Francis Joseph Fitzgerald, together with

Constable Richard O'Hara Taylor, Constable George Francis Kinney and their guide, Special Constable Sam Carter. The four set out December 21st but they never made it to Dawson. The trip became known as The Lost Patrol. This tragedy has spawned a number of tales and books, and a few songs; one of which, *Fly Like an Eagle* by the Gumboots, a group from Yellowknife, is very evocative of this tragic event. (See note on page 254.) We found the graves and spent a few minutes there, thinking about those long-gone days when it was so easy to get lost in the wilderness, and thought even today it would not be difficult to lose one's way in the wildness of these lands.

The graves of the Lost Patrol in the Anglican cemetery

After our visit to the gravesite it began raining a little, so we had lunch in the RV in parking lot of the Northern Store. This chain can be found all over the North. We had explored the stores in Moosonee, Inuvik and Tuktoyaktuk and always enjoyed their eclectic mix of commodities, from groceries to drugs to toys to clothes, and anything else you can think of.

By now it was early afternoon and the weather was a little damp, so we decided to continue the drive to Eagle Plains and stay there for the night. After our earlier experiences crossing the Peel River, we were curious to see how much it had changed. Thankfully, it was much easier as the ramps had had time to dry out and firm up. Now it was plain sailing to Eagle Plains. At the border of the Northwest Territories and Yukon we set our watches back to Pacific Time. The constant changing of the watches really brings home how huge this country is and how many times zones there are from sea to sea.

We couldn't resist stopping to take this picture of Meech Lake

Driving back towards Eagle Plains we came upon a number of trucks going our way, all from the same company and traveling together. These were the trucks we had first seen in Eagle Plains, and again in Inuvik a few days previously. They had brought up the heavy equipment for a military exercise, and were now returning empty. As always, being respectful of the gravel they could throw up and the potential damage this might cause, we stopped several times to allow them to pass us safely. When we neared the Arctic Circle marker we realized this must have been their first trip to this area, as they had obviously stopped there to record the experience. As they were all pulling out, I stopped and let them leave as a group, and was rewarded with a wave. Later on we spoke to one of the drivers in Eagle Plains and he said he appreciated that little courtesy.

Smooth, even sections of the Dempster Highway were a pleasure to drive

Our major excitement on this part of the drive was a caribou herd we came across, grazing some distance from the road. We had been told about this herd when we drove north, but we had not been able to see it. This time the caribou were out on the tundra and we stopped to admire them. We were thrilled to see the herd, albeit at a distance, and took a few (not very good) pictures.

As we drove a little further on we came upon the reality of caribou in the North. There were a couple of pickup trucks parked beside the road and some guys on the tundra pulling something towards the road. They had been hunting caribou and were hauling the carcase back to the trucks. We had eaten caribou ourselves and knew it was an important food source for the people of this area, but to go from the romance of seeing the herd to the reality of the herd providing food for a family was something we had to get our heads around.

A caribou herd at the extreme reach of our camera

Finally, we arrived in Eagle Plains and parked the van for the night. We met the lady from Montreal again. She had taken one of the ferries and had been taking pictures of everything she could. A little while after she left the ferry, she found she no longer had her camera, so she drove back to the ferry and was met by the captain. He had rescued the camera and realizing the importance of it, was wondering how to get it back to her. Such is the way of the North. She was extremely grateful, since she had a number of priceless pictures that had not been downloaded to her computer.

In the parking/camping area at Eagle Plains was a bizarre contraption, a bus with sleeping compartments in high-rise fashion, Das Rollende Hotel. This is a tourist bus with a difference. The company offers tours all over the north of Canada and Alaska in the summer, and then visits various places in the South and Central America in the winter. The buses are equipped to sleep 25 people, traveling during the day and booking into campgrounds overnight. There is a fully equipped kitchen with a cook who provided meals for the group on a regular basis. This particular bus was only going as far north as the Arctic Circle marker and then returning to Dawson City.

Das Rollende Hotel

Ghost bikes: what a good spray of Dempster mud will do if you attach your bikes to the back of the vehicle without a cover

Just for a change, we had supper at the Eagle Plains restaurant instead of in our RV, and were pleasantly surprised at the quality of the food. We took our desserts back to the RV and worked out our plans for the next few days. We intended to drive back to Dawson City and spend a couple more days there as tourists, and then cross the Yukon River and drive into Alaska. As we reflected on our trip so far—three weeks and counting—we were amazed at how much we had seen and learned and discovered, and how disconnected we felt from our 'real' life in Ottawa. While we did email and text family and friends, this experience was now our reality and home was the RV.

Our abiding memory of Eagle Plains is the rain. When we awoke the following morning we were not surprised to see it had been raining all night. So, after filling up with gas, we were on our way back to Dawson. We were surprised to see Das Rollende Hotel filling up and heading back the same way. The guests must have had an early start since it appeared they had already been to the Arctic Circle and back. As we left Eagle Plains the roads were muddy and sloppy again, and our friendly potholes had taken this opportunity to multiply and grow, which made for some interesting driving. Happily, the road conditions soon improved and the surface became more manageable, which gave us a much better driving experience this time around. We played an amusing game of tag with Das Rollende Hotel; it would pass us and then stop for a scenic look off, and we would re-pass it, and it would stop and... Eventually, the bus left us far behind on its way to Dawson City.

The road varied between some good surfaces where we could drive at highway speeds, and potholes and nasty surfaces. We were able to see things this time around that we had missed coming up, or perhaps there was so much to see that it was impossible to remember it all. At one point a Black Bear casually crossed the road, and it didn't move fast, even when it saw us approaching. After all, we were in his territory. The scenery continued to fascinate us and we kept looking around in wonderment. Even in the brief time we had spent in Inuvik I had forgotten how overpowering the mountains were, and how they grow as you get closer to them and in among them. There were many avalanche areas; we saw piles of loose rocks at the feet of all the mountains where they had slipped, and there were frequently trees and bushes at odd angles just sitting in various places where they had ended up. This was a very different and rugged world and one that was relatively new to both of us.

We arrived at the end of the road having driven 1500km from the start of the Dempster Highway to its end and back, and felt we had done something very special. It wasn't just the road conditions and the difficult driving—although they played a huge part—but the understanding of the importance of the highway to the people of the area and the effect on them when it becomes impassable.

Arriving in Dawson City we found the main campground was full, so it was off to the ferry to find a campsite in the territorial park on the other side of the river. After a peaceful supper at our campsite we went for a walk to find the water pump. And pump it was! We had to work hard to get the water out. There was a boil-water advisory, and since the water came directly out of the bottom of the Yukon River we understood why. It was brown and muddy and not very appealing to drink. Fortunately, we were only going to use it for flushing the toilet, so it really wasn't the concern it could have been.

After breakfast we went back onto the ferry across the Yukon to our original campsite in Dawson City, and prepared for a few more days of exploration. Having seen the *SS Klondike* in Whitehorse we were anxious to visit the *SS Keno* here in Dawson.

The *SS Keno*, which was built in 1922, is representative of the old paddle steamers of the Gold Rush period which were described as the work-horses of the Yukon. This family of steamers is unable to tow barges due to the stern wheel, so barges are pushed in front of the ship. The main task of this particular type of steamer was to push barges of silver/lead ore upriver to Whitehorse, as well as bringing supplies back down to Dawson, so this was a very different looking vessel from the rather grand *SS Klondike*. No fancy staterooms and accommodations on this paddle wheeler, but hard chairs and basic accommodations for travelers on the river.

The SS Keno *in Dawson City*

The captains of these riverboats needed to be very skilful in order to make it up and down the river in one piece, and each one had his own maps of the river. One of these maps was on display and included added comments and descriptions of the river in somewhat individual ways. The more obvious challenges like rapids and the ever-changing sandbars were marked, while other areas were identified by comments such as 'one tree on a rock'. I imagined sailing on such a ship, and thought about the issues faced both by the boat crew and the passengers.

After visiting the *Keno* we went to the Palace Grand Theatre, which was built in 1898 and functioned for many years entertaining miners when they came into town. It also did a good job in separating the miners from their gold!

An historical re-enactment at the Palace Grand Theatre

The show we attended was designed to include the audience and to provide information in a fun way about the Gold Rush era. Three actors represented three personages of the era (William Ogilvie, Klondike Kate and Mme Tremblay) describing themselves and their accomplishments during this period, and taking questions from the audience. After each person had spoken, audience members voted for who they thought was the most 'important and best' personage of the Klondike Gold Rush era. It was a wonderful way to introduce some of the history of the area, and to demonstrate how each person had played an important part in the lives of those living in Dawson at that time. On this day Ogilvie won by popular demand but, who knows, on another day it might be one of the others; they were all important figures of the time.

The Commissioner's Residence was now open. Our friend Mike Gates had been the team leader of the conservation and restoration work of this beautiful building, as it would have looked in 1912-16, when it was occupied by Commissioner George Black and his wife Martha. This project took eight years from start to finish and was finally completed in 1996. It was really exciting to see the result of this huge task. The building itself was interesting and we spent a happy hour or so there. After our tour we chatted to one of the docents, who knew Mike and Kathy back when they were living in Dawson. This was not surprising given the size of the town and the influence our friends have had on the cultural activity of region.

The Commissioner's Residence is restored and furnished to represent the period 1912-16

We learned more about the history of the area in another very entertaining way with a visit to Diamond Tooth Gertie's for a drink and the floor show. Although today this is a modern-day gambling establishment, it maintains the old look of the Klondike era. The burlesque shows are the main attraction, but the gambling and booze also play a big part in the success of this establishment. The waitresses were dressed in clothes reflecting the fashions of the Gold Rush era, which contrasted nicely with the modern shoes more appropriate for their work. While we were there Bob reminisced about his visit there in 1996 when he had spent some time chatting to an old prospector and checking out the nuggets of gold he had for sale.

Diamond Tooth Gertie's

The stage was in the main part of the establishment but, of course, like all modern casinos, we had to pass through the gaming area to get to the stage. It was a small stage, with many small tables for guests scattered around the main floor, and an overlooking balcony. We were seated near the front of the stage area, and settled in with a drink to enjoy the show. The place was packed with tourists just like us, who were interested in enjoying an old time burlesque show. We later learned this show was quite mild compared with the ones later in the evening, which became more risqué. As with all establishments of this nature, there were steely eyed men who walked around the place... just looking. They were well dressed in suits and ties and there was no doubting their job.

After the show we slowly walked back to the campsite and heard country music playing. We went to investigate and found a group of musicians just sitting around their trailers and jamming with accordion, banjo and guitars. They were all good players so we stayed and listened for a while. We wondered if they had attended the annual Dawson City Music Festival, which occurred while we were in Inuvik, but we didn't think to ask. As we went to sleep that night we could still hear the sounds of a guitar playing quietly in the campground. It was a lovely end to a very full day.

We had one more day of adventures in the North of Canada before leaving to drive the Top of the World highway into Alaska. Even though we wanted to do and see as much as we could in Dawson, our first priority had to be yet another car wash; it had become quite the theme in this part of the world. We were quite ashamed of our RV and wanted it to look at least reasonable before continuing our travels. Once the vehicle looked cleaner we drove a little way out of Dawson to visit Dredge Number 4. The dredge is an amazing structure. It floats on water and picks up gravel on a continuous bucket chain, crushes it and washes out the tiny nuggets of placer gold. This was the commercial way of extracting gold and meant the dredges worked 24 hours a day, creating the huge piles of rock or tailings we had noticed when driving into Dawson City.

While we were driving back from visiting the dredge we caught a glimpse of an animal to the side of the road. A fox obligingly posed for us before scuttling way behind the pile of rocky debris.

A fox obligingly poses for its picture

A wooden Parks Canada panel describing the dredge and a view of its business end

The Cremation of Sam McGee, the evocative poem by Robert Service, the Bard of the Yukon, is celebrated in Dawson City, along with many of his other poems. We had the opportunity to visit the cabin Service lived in during his time in Dawson. His many tales and poems about the Yukon were derived from all the stories he picked up from miners. We happily listened as a docent/interpreter described Robert Service, interspersing the story with poems that illustrated his life. It turned out that he didn't spend much time in the Yukon at all, but this didn't appear to have affected the popularity of his poetry.

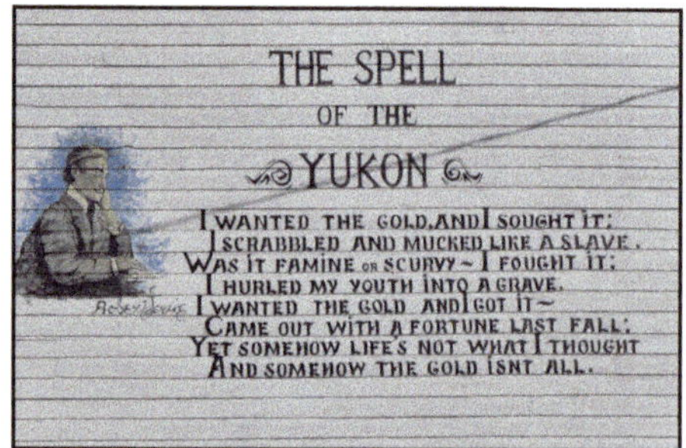

The cabin Robert Service occupied and one of his poems on a wall

Our last activity of the day was a drive up to the Dome overlooking Dawson City and beyond. The Dome may be classified either as a large rock or small piece of mountain with very winding road going up. At the top the visitor is rewarded with a bird's eye view over the whole region, impossible to catch with a mere photograph, but we still tried. Bob climbed up the very highest part of the Dome and met a couple who were higher than kites on pot. There was a lively discussion of the financial and taxation implications of legalizing marijuana. Bob was offered a toke but he politely declined!

The Yukon River looking north from the top of the Dome

Another view from the Dome looking upriver towards the south

We spent the evening getting ready for the next day's departure, then chatted with Bob and Claudia, a couple from New Brunswick parked in the next campsite. We had a lovely conversation during which we discussed our travel plans, and found out that they were leaving the next day and taking the same route as us. She didn't drive at all, so he had done all of the driving, which we found amazing since they had come even further than us. After supper we heard the musicians jamming once more, so ended the day listening to them while wondering what the next part of our trip would bring.

The campsite jam session

July 25th to July 28th

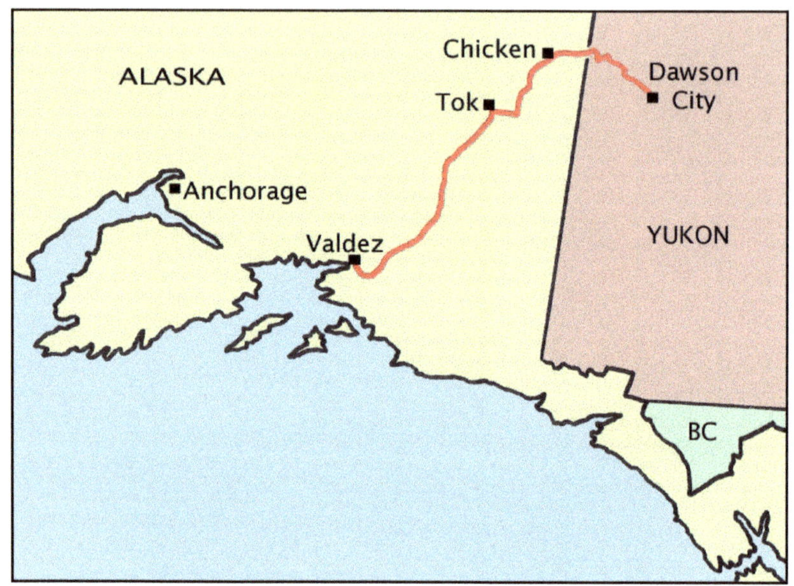

Dawson City to Chicken	173km
Chicken to Valdez	531km
TOTAL	704km

Chapter Eleven

Valdez via the Top of the World Highway

It was time to say goodbye to the Yukon and the Northwest Territories; we were ready to head into Alaska. We decided to take our time going towards the ferry, just to avoid the morning rush, or so we thought. The ferry across the Yukon is very small, and it seemed that every other RV or trailer in Dawson was planning to leave at the same time, which meant we were stuck in the ferry line-up for 30 minutes or so. We spent the time catching up with our friends Brett and Sandy who had just arrived from Inuvik, and also chatting to our New Brunswick friends from the previous evening. Finally, it was our turn to load. Bob had stayed with the RV while I was chatting with people way up the line, so when he began loading I had to walk very rapidly in order to get aboard. The ferry staff were amused and assured me they would have brought me across on the next ferry.

The second part of our trip had now officially begun. We were driving to Alaska via the Top of the World and Taylor Highways, eventually joining the Alaska Highway across the border at Tetlin. This was our second road having many stories told about it, both good and bad. While we had heard it could be quite rough to drive, it was reported to have some of the most spectacular scenery we would ever see, and it definitely lived up to both descriptions. We drove off the ferry and headed immediately uphill, confident that it could not be as bad as the Dempster, and we had survived that road quite well. So how much harder could this one be? Well, we found out! This road was very different in nature from the Dempster, and threw extra challenges our way.

Like so many of the roads we drove in the North the surface initially appeared good, but then the true roadway showed up and hard-packed gravel and potholes become a fact of life. It was difficult driving and harder than the Dempster because the road was much narrower and not as well maintained. We were surprised because we didn't think it was possible any major, well-traveled road could rival the Dempster. We did wonder if this was because the Dempster is a lifeline and vital trucking route, while the Top of the World Highway is basically a tourist road. It is closed during the winter months, and thus does not justify the same level of maintenance.

You really do feel as if you are on the top of the world and looking down

As always, we stopped several times to take pictures of the wonderful views. The scenery lived up to the hype; it truly was spectacular. At one look-off we were chatting with Bob and Claudia, our neighbours from the previous night, and noticed the tiny tires on their pop up trailer. We both thought it was a good thing they had not tried the Dempster, since we doubted the trailer was up to the task. They left a few minutes before us while we were still absorbing the view, and then we followed them up the road. As we were driving I noticed a corrugated pattern in the middle of the road ahead of us that reminded me of centre line markings, but not very likely on this road. Bob suggested that what we were seeing was rubber left by a rapidly deteriorating tire, and this turned out to be correct. We came upon our neighbours parked on the side of the road with a shredded trailer tire. We stopped to offer them some help. Bob got out our jack and started work, and I supported Claudia, who was quite upset, as the two men worked on the trailer. It wasn't an easy task as the wheel nuts were frozen tight, and neither of them had a long enough wrench to get leverage. But, as normal in the North, several more families with RVs had stopped to help, and with all that support and combined toolkits, the wheel was changed for the spare. It was a very happy ending for all concerned. So our erstwhile neighbours were now able to continue their travels, while Bob and I took a few moments to have lunch before continuing.

Roadside repairs and a view of the road ahead

The road continued to be difficult to drive, and while the roadbed did not become any better, the views certainly did. The day was so clear that we could see for miles and miles over all those mountains, and it really felt as if we were traveling across the top of the world. Finally, at what felt like the very top, we arrived at the US border with a signboard that read

'Population 2'. As we went through customs the officer asked where we were headed. "Valdez," we replied, to which he said, "Oh, yeah, Val-disease. That's what my son calls it 'cos it's so far from Anchorage." We were curious about the population marker so we asked him about that. His reply was short and to the point, "Yep, and I'm one of them." A lonely post at the furthest north crossing point between Canada and the United States.

Near the highest point of the highway

At this point the Top of the World Highway has an elevation of 1376m, and since we had made it up to the top we now had to come down again. We were heading towards Chicken, our planned stop for the night. On the US side the road became narrower and more winding, with many nasty downhill pieces and not a guardrail in sight! It reminded us a little of driving in the Alps, where the roads looked like spaghetti and the only thing between you and the side of the mountain is a length of string between two posts. There were stretches of downhill curves where I would have welcomed even a little piece of string along the edge. The Top of the World Highway joins the Taylor Highway at the turn-off for Eagle, but the change of name did not improve the condition of the road down to Chicken, where we were stopped for the night. As we drove into the town we passed the notice board proudly displaying the population of 30. This was quite the population compared to the US Customs Post, but it did serve to emphasize how few people actually live in this vast area.

A giant chicken greets the traveler to Chicken. The story goes that the town is so named because the founders couldn't spell Ptarmigan

Bob and Claudia invited us out to dinner that evening as a thank-you for our help and support with the trailer wheel. Given the population of Chicken, there were very few places to eat, but we did find a small café which was serving—you guessed it—chicken. The food really wasn't the important thing; it was the gesture, and we had a wonderful time just chatting. The talk turned to curling, and we learned Bob had been a competitive curler in his younger days, and had many interesting stories to tell about the curling world. All too soon it was time to go and prepare for another day of driving. Bob and Claudia were planning to drive down to Haynes

Junction, and it was our fervent wish their trip would be safe with no more flat tires on their little trailer. We were heading in a different direction, towards Valdez and the Pacific Ocean.

We left Chicken in the morning and headed west on the Taylor Highway. The driving finally became easier, and the views continued to be spectacular, with lots of snow-capped mountains in every direction. We drove through Tetlin and into Tok, where we stopped for lunch and went to the visitor centre. We picked up more tourist information, then joined the Richardson Highway heading towards Valdez, via the Tok cut off. *The Milepost* was our travelling friend and ally; with all the maps and excellent information provided we were now much more confident in our travels.

The scenic stop on the Richardson Highway

The mountain scenery continued to open out in front of us. At one beautiful scenic pull-off beside a lake we stopped for a break... and had an amazing encounter. Three rented RVs filled with German tourists had stopped ahead of us. They were talking amongst themselves, and at one point one of them used our wing mirror to steady his camera. We laughed, and Bob stepped over to speak with them. He was wearing his 'Rostock 2004' trumpet-making workshop T-shirt. It's the only one with Rostock written on it, and commemorates the first of many workshops Bob has offered with his friends Rick and Michael. The conversation was all in German: "Rostock!" one of them said. "We are from Rostock!" Bob told them he taught a workshop with his colleagues at the Handwerkskammer. "What is your colleague's name?" "Michael Münkwitz." A lady joined the conversation, "Oh, yes, Münkwitz! We know of him." "Yes", says another guy, "a friend of mine made a trumpet at this workshop." All of this in the middle of Alaska. It really is a small world!

After saying goodbye to our new German friends, we were off to Valdez. Once more the road became part of our adventure. At one point it was being 'fixed', so we waited for about 15 minutes and watched dump trucks pouring large gravel and rocks onto the surface to fill it in. Presumably, this section of road had been washed out. We finally passed the construction area only to be met with another one a few kilometres further down the road.

Eventually we came to the Worthington Glacier and pulled over and stopped in a well-maintained parking lot. This was our first experience of a glacier on this trip, and we were not quite sure of what to expect. There were nicely laid out paths leading from the parking, so we were able to get close to the foot of the glacier. There before us was saw a river of ice just sitting there and brooding, while allowing trickles of water to escape. Awe inspiring would be one way of describing it. We just stood there and marveled at what we were seeing.

The approach to the Worthington Glacier on well-made paths

The river of ice creeping into the valley

On our way back to the parking lot we met one of the staff on site. We were wondering how far this particular one had retreated, and learned that over the last 30 years it had gone back about 300m. It left us wondering whether this was part of the normal glacier cycle, or was it related to climate change?

We headed to Valdez over the Thompson Pass. This pass is reported to be one of the snowiest places in Alaska, and as we drove up and over we saw residual snow and ice from earlier falls. The Pass itself tops out at 2805ft (855m) and once over it, it was straight down to Valdez at sea level. We dropped over 2000ft in about nine miles (14.5km). Finally, we had a road that was economical in gas usage! As we approached Valdez we passed several waterfalls with such apt names as Bridal Veil and Horse Hair.

Bridal Veil Falls beside the road through the Thompson Pass

At last we were in Valdez. We soon found the Bear Paws Campground very close to the harbour and settled in. We were amused to learn we had been put in the Adult Park. We were not sure why, and had lots of ideas, most of which were not polite, but as it was so close to the waterfront it may have just been a safety feature. Whenever we could find WiFi service on our travels we hooked into it, and were amused to learn the security code at this campsite was 'seethebunnies'. When we parked the RV we found that the campground was overrun with large and small black bunnies. It explained a lot.

Black rabbits were everywhere in our campsite

We thought it would be interesting to take a sea cruise from Valdez and see some glaciers from the sea, along with any marine life that cared to show itself. Once we had settled in the campground we booked a wildlife and glacier tour of Prince William Sound. As we boarded the boat next morning we again met the Australian couple we had seen so long ago in Dawson City. After catching up with all the news, we went out on deck to see what Prince William Sound had to offer.

The weather was perfect when we left the dock, sunny with some fog patches on the mountains, and totally picturesque. Throughout the whole tour the captain provided an ongoing commentary on everything from the wildlife, to the history of the earthquake, to the oil refineries, to the *Exxon Valdez* oil spill, all of which we found very informative. He also told us about the glaciers and their patterns of growing and receding, and pointed out that the Columbia Glacier is receding while the Mears Glacier has grown visibly over the last few years.

Our first sighting of wildlife while still in the outer harbour of Valdez: a Bald Eagle sitting nicely in a tree just waiting for the photographers to take its picture

Once we were out in Prince William Sound, the porpoises showed up and played in the bow waves of the boat. According to the captain, they like the bow waves because they can surf on them, and it certainly seemed as if they were hanging about the boat and enjoying jumping in and out of the waves. Our next joy was the sea otters, just lying about and floating in the ocean. The mother otters looked so cute with their babies lying on their tummies. A little while later we spotted a whole colony of otters near a moraine left by the Mears Glacier many years ago. Apparently the otters like it there because the water is shallower and they are able to hunt for food more easily.

A porpoise surfs beside the boat and a mother otter with baby floats by

The first glacier visited on this boat trip was the Columbia, which is huge and deep and frequently calves. We didn't get very close to it, but its ice field made up for this. There were many floating chunks, but apparently on this day the ice field was considered small. We could see the glacier in the distance where it entered the sea about 18 miles away, and even though this glacier is receding it still looked huge. We continued to the Mears Glacier, and on the way we were fortunate to see a variety of birds, both in the water and in the sky.

The floating glacier ice is remarkably blue and comes in weird shapes

On our approach to the Mears Glacier it was difficult to comprehend the size of it until our guide told us that the tiny brown objects we could see right at its base were Harbour Seals. Then the scale was suddenly established. The captain brought the vessel very close to the edge of the ice, and held it there for some time. It was a wonderful experience to be this close to the ice wall. As we drifted through the ice and water we just watched and listened. The noise was ongoing and varied in intensity but, as the captain said, if you hear a crack it's too late; a lump of ice has already fallen. The speed of sound sees to that. This glacier is growing, and we could see the damage to the vegetation and trees done by the ice as it grew. This year alone, the glacier had extended many feet, and perhaps where we were floating might actually be solid ice in a year or so.

The Mears Glacier from some miles away as we approached

To give a sense of scale, the tiny dots at the base are Harbour Seals

Harbour Seals basking on the ice in front of the Mears Glacier

We were hoping to see whales on this trip, but this was not to be. The fog came down, and the whales did not show themselves. Our final excitement was a sea lion colony on the return leg of the trip. These were mainly young males, and they were very loud. We laughed, imagining them boasting about all their conquests, their muscles, the food they caught! It was very foggy, but our captain brought the boat as close in as he could, so we could see and hear them better. At one point there were three sea lions poking their heads out of the water, just checking what was going on, or were they posing for the camera?

Three sea lions pose for my camera

We sailed back into the harbour and spotted a pair of Bald Eagles sitting on a branch together, which was a great way to finish our wildlife tour. As we traveled through the harbour our captain/guide talked about the *Exxon Valdez* disaster and the procedural changes that have been made because of it. Now clean-up equipment is immediately available, and the rules and regulations about entering and leaving port have been tightened up considerably, so it is to be hoped there will never be another disaster like that one. After about six hours at sea we were back on dry land having had an experience we would never forget.

A pair of Bald Eagles giving the closing touch to our tour

Having had such a wonderful time in Prince William Sound, we now had to face reality and start planning for our travel in the general direction of Haines, Alaska. After all, we had a ferry booked for August 4th, less than a week away. We decided to go via Anchorage, so just to make the trip more interesting we would take the ferry to Whittier, and drive to Anchorage from there. Our first port of call was the tourist information centre to check the ferry schedules to Whittier the next day.

We were told we would need to go to the Alaska Marine Highway ferry terminal and book there. Since it was only five minutes away from our campsite we weren't too concerned.

While we were at the information centre we met some very frustrated German tourists. They had rented two RVs, one of which had got a flat tire while parked in their campsite up in the Thompson Pass. The 'toolkit' provided by the rental company had a totally inadequate jack and the wrench for the wheel nuts was the wrong size. So, with their very inadequate English they had been trying to contact the rental agency, which wasn't answering phones on the weekend, and towing services that also seemed to be taking two days off. Not a very good way to treat guests to the country.

Bob was able to discuss the problem with them, and he offered to help them out since we were carrying a decent jack and the correct wrenches. We completed our chores and about an hour later went back up the Thompson Pass in the pouring rain and found their campsite. Bob got out the equipment as soon as we arrived and, together with the two men, this well-drilled team got the job done in a very short time, although thoroughly soaked from the downpour. While the men were all working, I was inside with the two ladies. They showed me their vehicle and I showed them ours, and all the places we had been visiting. We had coffee and Martina gave me her card. She runs a small pension in Dresden and invited us to contact them if we are ever there. Who knows, maybe we will? As we left they gave us a nice bottle of wine as a thank you for helping them.

We returned to our campsite in Valdez to prepare ourselves for an early start the next morning, and enjoyed the wine with our supper.

July 29th to August 1st

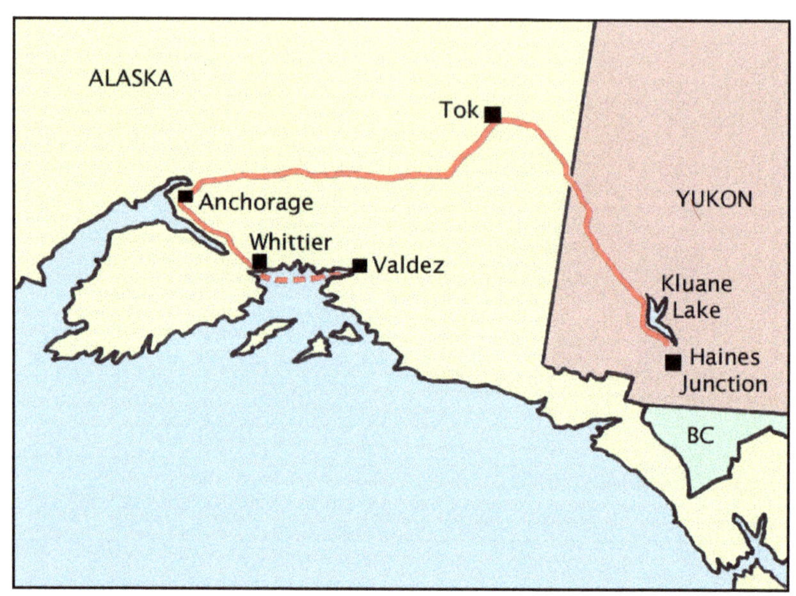

Whittier to Anchorage	97km
Anchorage to Tok	509km
Tok to Kluane Lake	309km
TOTAL	915km

Chapter Twelve
Valdez to Kluane Lake

New adventures now awaited us. We arrived at the ferry terminal at the unreasonable hour of 6:00am and after a re-measure of the RV (it's actually 9″ longer than we had been told) we were loaded onto the ferry. The ferry crew tagged the propane tank, presumably to prevent it being opened and, to our surprise, our small bottles of propane for the barbeque had to be stored in a hazardous materials storage locker.

We were sailing on the *MV Aurora*, which had played a huge part in the clean-up after the *Exxon Valdez* oil spill. The vessel had been a floating base for the personnel working on the clean-up, feeding and housing them, doing laundry and anything else that was needed. They also kept all the accounts necessary for the powers-that-be in the Alaska Ferry Service, as bureaucracy always rears it ugly head. The crew of the *MV Aurora* received commendations for all their work and support during this very difficult and distressing time. Learning about the practicalities of coping with this disaster was fascinating, and something not really known to the rest of the world at the time. We felt this kind of information should be shared as it exposes the human side of any drama.

This was our first long ferry voyage on this trip, scheduled to take 5 hours 45 minutes, which was approximately 5 hours 40 minutes longer than the ones we had been taking in the Yukon and Northwest Territories. We were sailing through fog for most of the time and what scenery we could see was shrouded. It was a very different view of this part of the world; almost mystical as little islands would suddenly peep out through the fog.

Islands appearing through the fog

We settled down in the salon and tried to watch for marine wildlife. Sea otters were plentiful; some swimming rapidly away from the boat, while others just meandered along in the ocean. Suddenly we noticed different wave patterns created by a couple of whales swimming far away from us; too far and too foggy to identify. Then Bob thought he saw some orcas, again too far away to be properly identified. Every so often the captain would point out things to the passengers, including a whale-watching boat and the whale they were watching. Bob and I saw the whale blow and dive with its flukes in the air, which was quite magical. Later in the day we spotted orcas swimming fairly close to the ferry, which was a joy.

Seabirds were constant companions on this mini voyage, and after the initial excitement they just became another part of the scenery. The ferry route passed the outflow from the Columbia Glacier, and this time the ice field was thicker than our previous experience. Some of the chunks were large enough to cause the ferry to manoeuvre around them. As we watched this we both recognized the dangers even these smallish icebergs may pose for shipping passing through these seaways.

After five hours we arrived in Whittier, and while the ferry was docking I chatted with a traveler from Inuvik and spoke about our experiences there. She appeared pleased to hear how much we had enjoyed our visit. Then it was time to disembark and find our way to Anchorage, our planned destination for the day.

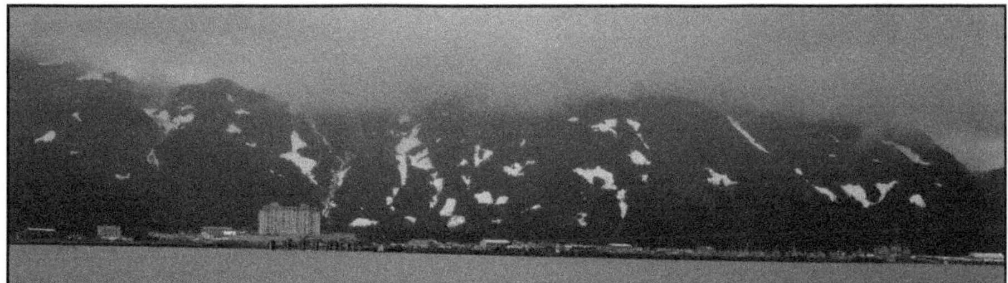

The approach to Whittier

The only road out of Whittier is through a tunnel. It's a rather odd tunnel—in fact, it's unique in the entire world—in that it shares its right-of-way with trains. It was originally a single track train tunnel and was later adapted so the roadbed occupies the same space as the train tracks. Trains have priority, so the traffic is stopped in four or five lanes reminiscent of a ferry line-up while a train passes through. We were fortunate to see a train leave Whittier and enter the tunnel. Once it was in the tunnel it was our turn to go through. Stop lights and an illuminated sign controlled the traffic; first buses and large trucks, then cars and finally RVs and similar vehicles. Once vehicles arrive near the tunnel portal a stop-and-go sign controls the spacing and timing; there's about 30 feet of space between vehicles and the speed is controlled to 25mph. It was disconcerting driving through the tunnel because the train tracks were slippery and tended to influence the steering. Having driven along streetcar tracks the sensation was familiar, but in Toronto you don't have rough-hewn rock walls on either side of you. Once this Anchorage-bound stream of traffic is through, it's the turn of the ones heading for Whittier, provided there's no train wanting to pass through. Unique indeed, and truly bizarre.

Sharing the road with a train

The final stretch of driving took us the short distance into Anchorage along the shores of Cook Inlet, an immensely wide arm of the sea. We had set our sights on Creekwood Campground, which had a very glossy advert in the Alaska travel brochure, but when we arrived it looked downright sleazy. We headed off to the tourist information office in town and got the names and addresses of a few more campsites. Ship Creek Landings sounded okay, so we headed there. If anything, it was worse... The third on the list was the Golden Nugget out by the Air Force Base and this, fortunately, proved to be quite decent. We caught the tail end of an air show, mostly war birds flying singly and in formation, and swooping over the town. As we were checking in we mentioned to the ex-pat Texan at the desk that we had tried those two other places and he said, "Yeah, that's the one I call Crackwood, and the other's Shit Creek."

Our new folding bikes had safely traveled with us all this time, so when we arrived in Anchorage, Bob decided to test his bike. He wanted to locate the Anchorage bike path network identified on the local map, and was able to find a little section of it before a soft tire forced a return to home base. We hoped, at some time during our stay in Anchorage, that we would be able to ride on the bike path that passes near Earthquake Park, and explore that area of the city. Unfortunately, due to a lack of time and poor weather, we were unable to do this, so the bikes were put away for another occasion.

We knew we could only spend one full day in Anchorage, and when we woke up and found the rain coming down, we decided to take the bus, the so-called People Mover (all-day senior's passes at $1.50 each) into the city centre. We arrived at the bus station without a map of the city and needed to find the visitor information center. We did get a little bit lost, so we asked a street sweeper the way. His name was Tyson and he set us on the right path and gave us information about Anchorage in general and told us to speak to Cyrus at the trolley stop: "He's the guy with the weird hat". He also told us that the best restaurant in town (perhaps in all of Alaska) is called A-K Gourmet. We found our way to the trolley stop (*left*) and booked two seats from Cyrus (in the weird hat) and did some gift shopping while we were waiting. We also went to the visitor centre, right across from Cyrus and the trolley stop, and picked up a map and other information.

The trolley took us on a one-hour tour of the city with the nice tour guide/driver telling us what we were looking at and the significance thereof. She had just married and her name was now Best, so she was the Best Tour Guide we could have had. The stop at Earthquake Park was shanghaied because there was a moose quietly grazing on the bushes in the parking lot. Great, we had traveled all these thousands of kilometres with scarcely a glimpse of moose, and there was one in the biggest city of Alaska.

The tour continued to the airport where we learned Alaska has the highest private plane ownership in the US. As we drove around we admired the planes, some with fat tundra tires, while others were float planes moored at the docks. Then the tour bus took us back to the town center. As we approached the trolley stop our tour guide finished with a beautfully sung version of the Alaska state anthem.

A moose grazing in Anchorage

We planned our afternoon activities over a coffee in Starbucks and then checked with Cyrus of the weird hat fame about the A-K Gourmet and asked where how to find it. His response was a disgusted, "That place? No way. Tyson has no taste!" So instead we headed off to the Anchorage Museum and the Cyrus-approved cafeteria. Given the rain, the museum seemed to be a good way to spend the afternoon, and we were in for a wonderful experience. This is an excellent museum with a very well laid-out and informative collection. The art gallery within the museum featured paintings and other artworks of Alaska, from the renditions of the artists who accompanied the first explorers to more modern works of the 19th and 20th centuries. The landscape works of Sydney Laurence were particularly fine, and it seems he had a real hankering for Mt McKinley (Denali) because there were several views of it, including one enormous canvas.

We wandered round an excellent display of native artifacts, which gave a sense of how people lived in this area before the continent was opened up by European and Russian explorers. It was a bit of a surprise to learn from one of the museum displays that the population of Anchorage makes up 46% of the population of Alaska. It did start to make sense when we considered all the apparently empty spaces he had driven through over the last few weeks. We returned to the campsite via the People Mover having seen some of the sights of Anchorage. Not bad for a rainy day in the city!

Our date with the ferry in Haines was coming closer. We had only four days and about 1300km to drive, while hopefully spending a couple of days in Haines before enjoying three days of peace (no driving) on the ferry. So, it was time to be on our way. We left Anchorage on the Glenn Highway and were soon surrounded by mountains and glaciers. We stopped at the huge Matanuska Glacier, which was easily seen from the highway, and as we drove away we could see it wind its way through the mountains. We also saw Tahneta Glacier, among others, from a distance but chose not to stop and look. It was fascinating to see these glaciers, especially as we now understood how they grow and recede, and could see the evidence of this.

The Matanuska Glacier seen from the Glenn Highway

Just for a change, this was the day we decided to treat ourselves to lunch at a restaurant in Glenallen instead of our usual lunch in the RV. We could only find one place to eat close to the highway, The Caribou Lodge, which looked quite nice. We sat down and Bob chose reindeer sausage in a bun, while I went for the crispy chicken salad. Twenty or so minutes after ordering we were informed that the reindeer sausage was no longer on the menu! Apparently no one had taken them out of the freezer that morning! So, Bob said he would have the same as me. After a while he noticed a plate waiting forever at the hatch to be delivered to a customer. He commented that, “Some poor so-and-so is going to get a cold meal.” We laughed and waited for our salads. Another 15 minutes or so passed, and we were finally served, and guess who got the cold lunch? Yes, it was Bob's. It was the original chicken salad that I had ordered, but because Bob's meal had been changed for no fault of his own, my chicken salad had cooled down and had then been served to him! We were not impressed by the service and even less so when we informed the cashier of this fiasco. All we received was an offhand, "Sorry!"

So away we went away, not hungry but very dissatisfied, and finally arrived at the Sourdough Campground on the Tok Cut-off, where we stayed for the night. What a contrast to our lunch! The campsite manager was happy to see us, and obviously enjoyed guests. He informed us of the pancake toss at 7:00pm; you could earn a free breakfast if you managed to toss a pancake into a bucket. It sounded like a lot of fun, so after supper we went over to try our luck.

The venue of the pancake toss, featuring photos of previous contestants and the buckets that act as the targets

The manager was a real entertainer, encouraging people, teasing people, really engaging the audience, and by the time it was all over three people had won a free breakfast. Bob and I were not part of that elite crowd; it was trickier than it appeared. Afterward, the manager hosted a campfire with marshmallows to the delight of all the children.

Before we left the campground the next morning we enjoyed a pancake breakfast and chatted with some of the other campers, one of whom had won her meal. We left after breakfast and headed to Haines Junction, Yukon. During much of this trip we had trusted Madame GPS to get us to places we wanted to go, and to tell us how long it would take. We would also check the route on a map as well, and this time was no exception. Madame advised us that this part of the trip to Haines Junction would take over six hours. Our immediate reaction was, "She's wrong, it's not that far!" However, she was right! We were back on the Alaska Highway, and like most of the roads we had been on, it began well but deteriorated fast, with the ongoing need for repairs to the surface, all of which required slow and careful driving.

At some point we noticed a rustling sound coming from somewhere in the camper. After stopping to examine the tires, which were just fine, we checked the rest of the vehicle and couldn't see anything wrong. The only conclusion to be drawn was that the duct tape on the roof might be coming loose. Considering the weather the vehicle had coped with since Beaverlodge, and the repair to the roof being almost a month old, this wasn't be surprising. So we drove for a couple more miles and stopped at an information area. There Bob climbed on a picnic table with the vehicle's leveling blocks piled on it, and was just able to see the repair. The duct tape was lifting, so he applied more where he could reach. When we were on our way again we could still hear the wind was rushing through the inaccessible part of the repair. At our next stop, a gas station, Bob was able to borrow a ladder, get up onto the roof and make yet more repairs with duct tape. We figured there was at least one, possibly two, rolls of duct tape holding it down. This all took quite a bit of time, so perhaps Madame GPS knew something we didn't.

After this mini adventure we were back on the highway only to be rewarded by being stuck behind two U-Hauls. Judging by their snail-like pace I thought they must be carrying Granny's expensive china and crystal in the back of them! After many miles we finally passed them, which created the next dilemma; how long do we drive before stopping for lunch, just in case they pass us while we're off the road? Eventually we took a chance and stopped at Pickhandle Lake.

This is a beautiful lake and we were only one of several campers who chose to stop here for lunch, including the owner of a dog called Hunter. Now, this lake was full of ducks and they hung around the area where the people were, waiting for handouts. After lunch we went out to see them and were treated to a wonderful show. Hunter was in the water chasing the ducks. A harmless occupation you may think, but the ducks were faster that he was, and they knew the lake, and Hunter was only interested in chasing them. As they went further and further out into the lake, the owner started to call, "Hunter, come here boy!" and variations on that theme. Hunter wasn't interested and went even further. I made a comment about the owner having to go in after the dog, something he definitely didn't plan to do. Gradually, Hunter was drawn back towards the shore by the ducks as they changed direction.

Hunter hunts the ducks

By this time the owner had his whistle out and was blowing it hard and fast. Hunter continued to ignore it; his focus was only on the ducks. As the ducks came closer so did Hunter, and as Hunter came closer his owner called and whistled more frantically. Finally, Hunter arrived wet and tired. This whole episode took about 10 minutes, but while the dog was shaking himself he spotted the ducks again and started to head back into the water! This time he did pay attention to his owner, came out very quickly and was rapidly put back into their truck. The owner's wife commented that the dog would sleep for hours after that swim!

After this amusing interlude we left the picnic area and started on our way again. The road was deteriorating once more, so we were stuck in many line-ups, and at one point we had to follow a pilot car through a construction zone. Finally, we made it through the road repairs and were on our way again, with the road still slow going but improving. I started looking for campsites as we approached Haines Junction and we found a beautiful place, Cottonwood Campground, where we stayed for the night. It is on Kluane Lake and our campsite was right at the water's edge, so we could hear the waves lapping at the shore.

Beautifully coloured wild grasses framed by Kluane Lake

It was a beautiful sunny afternoon so we went for a walk around the campsite and just enjoyed the ambience. After supper the wind started getting up and the appearance of the lake was totally transformed. A flat, peaceful body of water with a tranquil surface became a vista of rolling waves with dark, looming sky. By the late evening the wind had picked up even more and at times shook the RV. Thankfully, the wind storm blew itself out during the night and we were able to have a restful sleep.

Before and after as a wind storm crosses the lake

August 2nd to August 7th

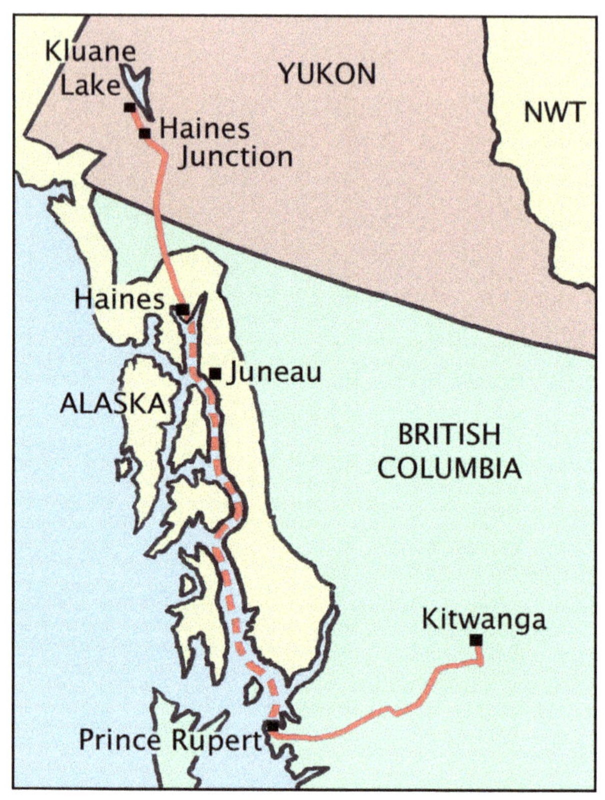

Kluane Lake to Haines	344km
Driving in Haines	72km
Ferry Haines to Juneau	5 hours
Driving in Juneau	25km
Ferry Juneau to Prince Rupert	2 days
Prince Rupert to Kitwanga	299km
TOTAL	740 km

Chapter Thirteen
Kluane Lake to Kitwanga

As we headed towards Haines Junction we were amused by a road sign: Beware of Cross Winds. No sooner had we read it, the winds picked up. Clearly, from our experience of the evening before, this was a predictably windy region. We passed a number of huge mountains and passes, lakes and rivers, and at one point a large cat—perhaps a lynx or mountain lion—crossed the road in front of us. This made a change from the deer we are used to in Ontario. Road maintenance continued to be a major story in our travels and we needed pilot cars on several occasions just to bring us safely through these areas. Our route took us through Haines Junction and a simple right turn put us on the road to Haines, Alaska. Now we were once more driving though wonderful scenery on a high plateau between mountains.

A pilot car leading us through yet another set of road works

We kept coming across groups of cyclists toiling up the mountain roads. They weren't carrying any equipment on their bikes, so we assumed they had a support vehicle somewhere, unlike the cyclists we had met in Inuvik who had ridden the Dempster. Even so, while we admired their stamina, we were glad we were using the RV's power to bring us up these mountains rather than pedal power.

The highway we were on follows much the same route as the Dalton Trail. The trail started in Haines, Alaska and went through the Chilkat Pass, finishing in Fort Selkirk, Yukon Territory. The highest point of the road is 3510ft about sea level, and we imagined those prospectors of the Gold Rush era walking up this trail until they found themselves in Fort Selkirk, where they took boats or rafts down the Yukon to Dawson City. We noticed signs along the modern-day highway commemorating Dalton who had driven his cattle from Saskatchewan to Dawson City during the Gold Rush to provide fresh meat for the miners, and made a great deal of money doing so. Passing through this area we saw that his choice of route made sense; we were driving through alpine meadows, which would have provided good feed for the cattle and would also allow them time to rest in a safe environment.

We drove straight down from the Chilkat Pass and into Haines, crossing the US/Canada border for the sixth time. We were amused by this, since it is all due to the geography of the two countries. To travel from Anchorage to Haines the driver has to exit the US and enter Canada in the Yukon, then leave Canada just before Haines and re-enter the US. As a result, the border guards of both countries seem very familiar with tourists.

The first point of interest for us, the Valley of the Eagles, occurred just as we entered Haines. This is a huge nesting place for Bald Eagles. The best time to see the birds in this area is between September and December when they come in to feed on the late run of Chum Salmon. We saw a single eagle as we drove through, but more than made up for it later in our stay here.

A Bald Eagle soaring over Haines

Haines is not a big city, and we were lucky enough to find a campsite right on the water, and on the road to the ferry dock. Having clarified our ferry bookings we were free to explore the town, so we gently ambled around just to get our bearings. Because of its size it is possible to see and do a lot without the need to drive.

We had one and a half days for exploring Haines before our ferry left. First on the list was the Sheldon Museum. To find a museum of this quality in a small town like Haines was a very pleasant surprise. It was housed in a new building, purpose-designed and with an excellent collection. The founder was an inveterate collector and on his death his heirs bequeathed his collection to the museum and found the money to house it. Given Bob's work in conservation services to museums, we spent some time talking with the curator and assistant, discussing collections care and museum services, which are quite good for these remote communities. A conservator from the Alaska Museum in Juno is available for consultations, and will visit if required. We discussed the Shotridge Blanket—a famous Chilkat blanket that was owned by one of the early natives at the time of the first European contact—now in the collection of the Canadian Museum of History. The Sheldon Museum has a letter of intent from the CMH to have the blanket come to Haines for display. At the time of writing there is still much paperwork, contracts, funding, etc. to be done before this will happen.

Our next visit was to the Hammer Museum. Stop laughing, there is such a place! In fact, there are two such museums in the world, one in Haines and the other one in Lithuania!

There were at least 1,800 hammers on display, and a big one outside

There were hammers for everything and anything, and we spent some time chatting with the museum's summer intern. Unfortunately, the collector wasn't on hand, but Bob suggested that the museum get a trumpet-maker's hammer and a *Clack*, which is a hammer-like device for neatly decapitating boiled eggs. Who knows if the owner will follow up with those suggestions?

Later that day we found ourselves at the Alaska Bald Eagle Preserve and were fortunate enough to meet a carver who was working on a couple of door posts for the museum. Although he was doing beautiful work, we were a bit disappointed that he was not Tlingit. While he did not discuss how he learned his carving skills, he was using the traditional tools and techniques, which at least allows the techniques to be passed on, if not the native tradition. Once inside the building we were in time to see a Bald Eagle being fed, as well as the two owls cared for by the museum staff. These birds, and others in their care, have been injured in some way and are unable to live in the wild, so this program provides a safe environment for them while allowing visitors the opportunity to see and learn about these beautiful birds.

Injured wild birds being cared for at the Alaska Bald Eagle Preserve

Finally came the culmination of our wildlife safari. On the advice of the staff at the Alaska Bald Eagle Preserve we drove nine miles to Chilkoot Lake on the look-out for Grizzlies. These bears, known as Brown Bears in this region, are quite common and frequently seen in that area. The lake and shallow river are full of fish and the bears often come down to feed here, facing competition from the anglers who also enjoy fishing. We stopped at a bridge at the mouth of the river and there was a bear just wandering about near the water. It was being admired by several people standing on the bridge who, like us, were amazed at actually seeing a Brown Bear in its own habitat. While we were admiring the bear we could see a number of guys fishing further upriver, and we wondered how this juxtaposition of bear and human impacts on the bear behaviour.

Our first sight of a Brown Bear

The bear we saw had an ear tag, indicating concerns about its behaviour, and didn't bode well for its longevity. But with all that, seeing a Brown Bear in the wild is an experience I won't forget in a hurry.

On our last day in Haines we needed to be at the ferry terminal at around 5:00pm, which left us lots of time to get organized and see more of the town. So after a quick trip to the visitor centre to get information about Juneau, we wandered off to the Farmers' Market which is held regularly on the State Fairgrounds. Many years ago the movie *White Fang* was filmed in Haines, and they created a set purporting to be a town of around 1900. It has now become a tourist attraction, the buildings being used as stores and boutiques, with the boardwalks still present, allowing patrons to access the buildings easily. It is very attractive to look at and fun to walk around. Bob was interested in the micro-brewery located in one of the stores, so we went to check it out. It was an interesting set-up, but unfortunately there was no beer to taste at that time of day. The Farmers' Market, held behind the movie set, was very typical example of its kind and we enjoyed checking it out but limited our purchases to some fancy rice.

With a couple of hours to spare we went back to the Chilkook Lake area to enjoy the view, have a cup of tea and, if we were lucky, catch sight of a bear. As it was 3:00pm we thought the chances of seeing a bear were very slight, but you never know. Driving up the road to the lake we again noticed the number of anglers wading in the river. With so many people in the water, we wondered how the bears actually managed to feed at all. It is not surprising they are becoming habituated to humans.

We parked the RV and were enjoying the sun and our tea, when a cry went up; a bear was wading up the river towards us. The crowd moved as one towards the river. The bank of the river was high at this point and was covered with foliage, so the bear would be several feet below the crowd. As we waited impatiently the bear appeared, wading in the water and obviously fishing. His nose was down and he moved his head from side to side, watching the water. We saw him curl his paw, swish it in the water, and pick up a piece of salmon. It appeared to be an off-cut of a fish someone had caught.

A Brown Bear fishing in the Chilkook River. He gave us a grandstand view

As we watched the bear caught and ate several little white fish. I don't know what kind they were, but he obviously enjoyed them. He was walking and swimming about in front of us for quite some time, but eventually climbed out of the water and disappeared into the undergrowth. After he was gone it seemed unbelievable that we had just watched a Brown Bear fishing for his supper.

After that wonderful experience, we drove back into town to visit the area where Fort Seward had been. We stopped by the parade ground and looked at houses from the late 19th century. There was a little road named Soapsuds Lane, which intrigued us since we knew there had to be a story behind it. Apparently, in the period when the fort was functioning, the wives of the NCOs would take in laundry to make some extra money, so the lane where they lived became known as Soapsuds Lane. As we wandered about we came upon a derelict building with some really well-made house poles and a wonderfully carved and painted front.

The disused community centre

The building didn't seem to be doing anything but returning slowly to nature, while beside it there were some totem poles lying on the ground. We spoke to a local carver in a workshop nearby. He was not Tlingit, but he was carving in their style, and it was from him that we learned that the building had been the community centre for the local native people, but gradually they had moved away to a different area outside Haines. The building was now very rarely used and had been left to disintegrate. A sad end to what must have once been a beautiful building.

On the way back we stopped by the harbour front to examine a steam drill on display. It had been used for taking core samples in the gold exploration days, and was now an open-air exhibit. A restorer was working underneath painting some parts when we showed up, and he turned out to be the owner of the Hammer Museum, so Bob had a short chat with him before we went on our way. It was time to head to the ferry terminal.

A steam-driven core drill used in gold exploration

The ferry trip to Juneau was five hours, but because it was late in the day there was little to see, and this made it seem much longer. We located some brochures about Juneau at the ferry information desk, and knowing we would be getting in late, we looked for campsites in the area. Once off the ferry I programmed Madame GPS with the address of a campground and she took us there in nine minutes, which was a blessing. Not only that, the owner of the campground was expecting people off the ferry and came out to greet us. She found us a campsite, gave us lots of information about Juneau, and sent us on our way. We found our spot, parked the vehicle and went to bed.

Having arrived in Juneau late at night we had nearly the whole of the next day to explore the city before boarding the ferry for Prince Rupert. The Mendenhall Glacier was only about a 10 minute drive from our campground, so we decided to go there right away. We were also interested to learn about the Black Bears that inhabit this area, rather than the more common Brown Bears found along the coastline.

As we strolled along the boardwalk leading to the glacier viewing point, we noticed a group of people clustered in one spot and staring up into a tree. Rumour had it that a Black Bear and her cub were asleep up there. They were all waiting to see if she would come down and show off, so we waited as well. All we could actually see, high in the canopy, was a black blob that occasionally moved, so after a little while we wandered off. As we crossed little stream we noticed it was full of spawning salmon. We watched as the females made holes for the eggs while the males just hung around waiting for the ladies to spawn. No wonder the Black Bears all hung around here.

Spawning salmon

Us framed by the Mendenhall Glacier and the Nugget Falls

The Mendenhall Glacier, spectacular even under grey skies

Mendenhall is a huge glacier, about 500m across and extending away back into the mountains. Like so many of the glaciers, this one is also retreating and the display panels allow visitors to appreciate the changes that have occurred over time. There were lots of quite large bergs in the water, which told us this glacier extended far under water in order to create such large lumps of ice. Close to the glacier, but separated from it, was the Nugget Falls. There was a trail to the waterfalls, which we decided not to follow, so we just admired the falls from the distance. We walked as close to the glacier as we could, reading the interesting interpretive panels along the way. On the way back to the vehicle we checked the black bear in the tree but she hadn't moved so we left her to sleep and drove into Juneau.

We located the Alaska State Museum, which we felt merited a visit, and spent several hours visiting the displays. There was an interesting exhibit about World War II in Alaska from 1942 onwards. The Japanese had landed on the Aleutian Islands and posed a serious threat to the continent. They were displaced a couple of years later by combined American and Canadian forces, and the islands were manned until the end of the war. This military action was the reason for building the Alaska Highway in 1942 to 1943. This route was used to transport troops and equipment from the lower states. We knew the US Army had built the highway, and now we had a clearer understanding of the circumstances.

The exhibit of Tlingit and Inuit history and artifacts in the Alaska State Museum is extremely good and includes some excellent carvings. The house posts and house fronts were particularly impressive. One strange thing we noted, both here and in Anchorage, is that the peoples of the Arctic areas are still referred to as Eskimos, while in Canada that term was dropped some time ago. An interesting cultural difference.

A short way from the museum we found a small farmer's market and bought some baked goods to supplement our supplies. Since we still had some time before returning to the ferry terminal, we followed the road sign: End of Road 24 miles. While we didn't make it to the end of the road, we did enjoy the scenery on the way. This signpost was a reminder of the unique position of Juneau as the State capital. It is not connected by road to the rest of the Alaska, and relies entirely on the ferries of the Alaska Marine Highway for all its road transport.

Once back at the ferry terminal we located our loading line and then watched the happenings on the ferry. It was interesting and reassuring to watch the crew conduct an anchor drill; we thought that at least they would be able to stop the ship if they needed too. Then cars, trucks, trailers and RVs were all rearranged just to get them into the right order for boarding.

Now it was time to board! The crew boarded a couple of cars, and then stopped. We couldn't understand why, but when we saw a mass of people coming through from behind our ferry, and cars coming through in front of us, we understood another ferry had docked and was being offloaded first. Finally it was our turn, but first, and much to our amusement, the few cars already loaded were now off-loaded. It became obvious those cars had been tidied out of the waiting line so that the other ferry's vehicles could exit first. It really is a complicated process organizing all these vehicles, and getting them on and off the ferries in a timely manner. Once the real loading started we were one of the first vehicles on, which meant we would be first off in Prince Rupert. We were parked by the stern watertight doors, together with another vehicle of about the same length, rather like the cork in the bottle. This meant that when the ferry docked in Prince Rupert, we would need to be ready to drive the RV off as soon as the doors opened. Otherwise we would be keeping all the other passengers waiting.

A typical ferry scene we would encounter many times on this trip

For this voyage we had booked a cabin as neither of us felt like sleeping in a chair for two nights. After all, we are no longer 20 years old and able to sleep anywhere! The cabin was small, but quite serviceable, with a washroom a bit larger than ours in the RV. There were two bunks, a lower one and an upper one with a ladder. Bob kindly took the top and I luxuriated in the bottom one. We went to the cafeteria for supper and another of those coincidences occurred. We started chatting to a couple, Chuck and Bonnie, from southern California, and much to our surprise they remembered us from Eagle Plains. They were there as we were going up to Inuvik, and Chuck and Bob had chatted briefly. They had only gone as far as the Arctic Circle because, unsurprisingly, they had concerns about the safety of their trailer on the Dempster.

It was time for an early night. We had forgotten this was a ferry, not a cruise ship, and much to our surprise and dismay, we were woken up at around 4:00am with the docking in Sitka, one of the ferry's usual stops. This was the first of several stops as the ferry serviced the remote coastal towns not accessible in any other way. After this early start to the day, things became more interesting. The scenery through the Inside Passage is spectacular; lots of beautiful islands, birds, fish and the occasional whale.

We did see a couple of Orcas, and there were reports of a Bowhead whale far-off, which we glimpsed as we docked at Petersburg, another of those ports the ferry regularly serviced. We had a choice of going ashore in some of these tiny places, as some of the passengers did, but we decided to stay aboard.

The best photo we have!

Harbour Seals enjoying the refuge of a buoy as the ferry entered Petersburg harbour

The ferry is a relaxing way of traveling. Somebody else is doing the 'driving' and there is time to socialize with new friends, and to see how families and couples choose to interact with each other, while at the same time maintaining a level of personal space. In the evening many of the older couples, including us, brought out games and cards, and quietly played their game of choice. It was neat to see the tables in the cafeteria being used for this, and to see the quiet concentration of the occupants as they focused on their particular game.

The mountain scenery through the Inside Passage is stunning

A sombre scene of a distant glacier. We saw very little sunshine and the weather remained cool and windy

After a second and more restful night we were into the last part of this voyage. We chatted with all our new friends and acquaintances and exchanged contact information with Chuck and Bonnie. We invited each other to park in our respective driveways if either couple were ever in the vicinity. They found Alaska Marine Highway jackets on sale in the ship's gift shop for only $20.00 each, so we each bought one, not just to keep us warm out on deck, but also as practical souvenirs of the journey. They have the advantage of being both warm and wind- and waterproof, and have been well used since in our Ottawa winters.

As the ship neared Prince Rupert we made sure to be ready to get down to the vehicle deck quickly once it opened, since our RV would be first or second off. It turned out that we were the second vehicle to disembark in Prince Rupert. As a result, we made it through the Canadian Customs and Border crossing very quickly; our 8th and last border crossing of the trip. Then, after doing some basic shopping in Prince Rupert, we headed east beside the Skeena River to a campground near Kitwanga, where we had planned to stay the night. It was a nice simple campground, and after supper we went for a walk around the site, chatted with a family from California, and then checked out the map for the next day's visit to both Kitwanga and Gitanyow. We had plans to visit two sites of famous totem poles.

August 8th to August 15th

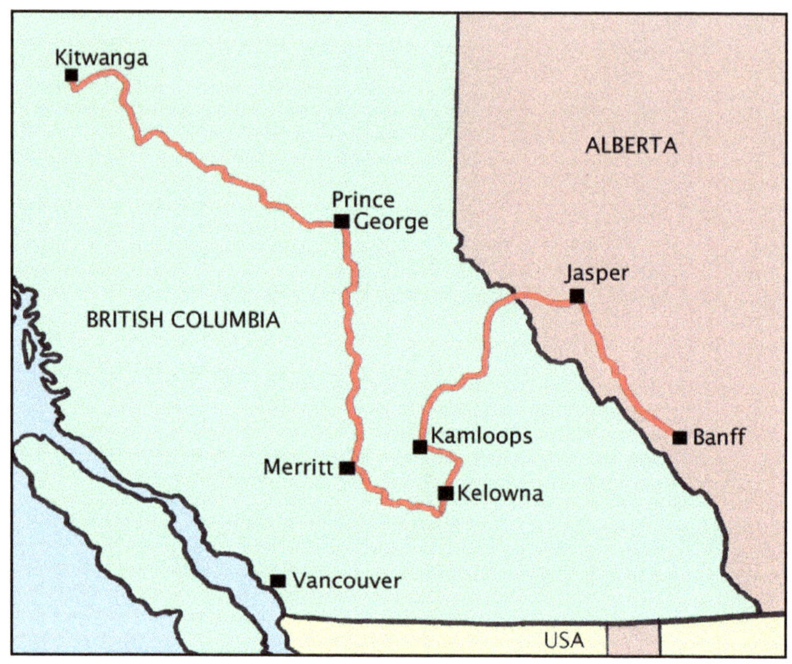

Kitwanga to Prince George	546km
Prince George to Merritt	551km
Merritt to Kelowna	137km
Kelowna to Jasper	612km
Jasper to Banff	305km
TOTAL	2,151km

Chapter Fourteen
Kitwanga to Banff

On our arrival in Kitwanga the night before we had briefly spotted the totem poles in the village as we drove to our campsite. We decided to visit Gitanyow first and then double back to Kitwanga before heading east again. The small town of Gitanyow is famous for its standing totem poles, the greatest concentration of original poles in British Columbia (and, by extension, the rest of the world) and Bob was anxious to see them. So we headed north up Highway 37, the Stewart/Cassiar Highway, to Gitanyow, or Kitwancool as it used to be called. We were amused to think that if we just stayed on this road we would eventually arrive in Watson Lake in the Yukon, which would make a complete circle! However, we chose to go only as far as Gitanyow and the totem poles, and then head south towards the Okanagan Valley.

We arrived in this small village and saw the poles, all 23 of them, standing in a field off the main street. They were all upright, although in various stages of deterioration. Some of the carving is quite spectacular, and even with erosion and deterioration over time, the sculptural quality is astounding. An information board provided by the Province of British Columbia described them as 'primitive art', which hardly does them justice; this work is far from primitive and shows a control of the medium and an artistic expression of enormous sophistication. It was clear that some effort had been made to preserve the poles—some are raised from the ground on concrete plinths, and many have reinforcing beams inserted into their hollow backs—but it also appeared the local people were not all that concerned about their wellbeing. There was a museum building on site, but it looked closed and bore all the signs of abandonment. Beside it was a half-finished pole, black with mould and slowly 'returning to nature'. It looked as if a brief cultural renaissance had lapsed. While the beauty of some of the poles was breathtaking, the overall impression was of grief and loss. We left Gitanyow feeling somewhat sad about the loss of a culture that seemed to be demonstrated by these poles, and traveled back to Kitwanga.

Tlingit totem poles at Gitanyow

Totem poles lining the main street in Kitwanga

There were fewer poles in Kitwanga but, as in Gitanyow, the artistry was of the finest. A couple of the poles were leaning at drunken angles, and two fallen ones had been dragged aside and allowed to rot. The carved surfaces were collapsing and the wood was soft, black and spongy. It is true that in the native peoples' ethos old poles should be allowed to fall and rot away and return to nature, thus completing a natural cycle, but sadly what we saw here and at Gitanyow was much more an expression of lost cultural identity. If the cycle was working as it should, there would be evidence of new poles being carved. There seemed to be no continuation of this tradition in either village unlike our experience in Alert Bay, where we saw some powerful expressions of cultural identity. As we left Kitwanga an attractive church caught our attention. We knew very little about the building, and we wondered why the bell tower was off to one side.

The isolated bell tower and the little wooden church in Kitwanga

The next stop was K'san near Hazleton, a reconstructed native village. This assemblage of longhouses was created in the 1970s during the great upswing of Canadian cultural identity surrounding the Centennial, although the buildings were on a much smaller scale than the actual houses would have been.

Reconstructed traditional buildings in K'san

The guided tour took us through three buildings containing artifacts associated with the traditional lifestyle. It was an audio presentation with the guide pointing out the objects and answering questions. It gave more insight into the traditional practices and beliefs, enhancing what we had learned years ago at Alert Bay. Outside one building was a half-finished pole rotting away, and the facades of the buildings needed attention. The guide told us that the regalia we had seen in one of the houses continues to be used at gatherings, although these are usually held in the larger community hall. It was heartening to know that the traditional observances continue, because there is the potential for so much to be lost. After a morning of visits involving native art and culture it was time to head south in the direction of Prince George. We passed though Smithers, where our son Ian had stayed on a school trip, saw a glacier off in the distance, and 'raced' a train of ore cars that shared a valley with us, and naturally lost the race since a train has right of way and doesn't need to stop for traffic lights!

A pleasant stop to watch salmon fishing while having lunch

This felt like a long day's driving; perhaps our restful time on the ferry had made us forget the driving aspect of this trip. We found a campsite just outside Prince George and, after we had settled in, a guy from the next campsite came over to talk to Bob. And what a curmudgeon he was! We figured he just likes to stay in campgrounds and just complain to people rather than actually see, explore and enjoy the world. He had nothing good to say about anywhere he had visited.

The next day saw us heading to Kelowna and seeing our long-time friend Gwen, who lived there. Happily, the driving was much easier, with good paved roads and thankfully no construction to hold us up, a wonderful contrast to the roads we had been traveling, both in Canada and Alaska. The weather also started to smile on us; it was sunny, albeit windy at times, and getting warmer. Now, finally, we had a chance to wear those shorts we had brought with us. The last time we wore them was the day before we arrived in Whitehorse, a full three weeks ago. As we drove down towards the south on Highway 97 so many things reminded us of where we had come from; if we had turned around and headed north the road we were on would eventually become the Alaska Highway at Dawson Creek.

One of the joys of this road was the many horses in the fields alongside the road. We were not sure what kind of horses they were, but since some places were offering trail riding, we guessed they were bred for that activity. We would have like to take a trail ride, but this didn't happen on this trip. Two years later we were able to fulfill that dream and take a trail ride in the canyons of Nevada.

As we continued further south the scenery changed from the lush growth we had so quickly become accustomed to, to arid desert-like scenery with lots of sand, sagebrush and not much else. The mountains on either side of the valley grew bigger and more rugged as the road wound through them. Soon we came upon a sign beside the road: Watch for Long Horn Sheep. I scanned the hills on both sides and saw no sign of them but then, right on the road itself, we came across two adult sheep and a lamb! They were running around a cyclist on the road ahead of us. (We just couldn't get the camera out in time.)

The vegetation changed quickly from lush green to scrub and sagebrush

We were heading towards Merrit for our evening stop, so we had to cross over the Thompson River at Spences Bridge. Once over the bridge, the road started climbing ever upward, which was both beautiful and scary at the same time. This was a very narrow road with many drop-offs and tight curves, but the scenery had to been seen to be believed; a river ran through the bottom of the valley, with farms and animals on each side of it. At one point we stopped at a look-off to enjoy the scenery, and while we were there a pickup truck and camper pulled over ahead of us. We drove by slowly, just to see if they needed help. Fortunately, they didn't because it was our friends from the ferry, taking the same route as us. Chuck and Bonnie had recognized us and stopped to say hello. It was a huge surprise because we knew they were on their way to Idaho, and traveling faster than us. So after a brief reunion we were both on our way again. We finally made it into Merritt and had a quiet evening in our campground, enjoying the warmer weather and the stream running through the site.

A beautiful steep-sided valley on the way to Merritt from Spences Bridge

We left Merritt early next day and were looking forward to arriving in Kelowna and seeing our long-time friend Gwen. But before that happy moment came we needed to take Highway 97C which goes over a range of mountains to the Pennask summit, then descends to West Bank on the Okanagan Lake. We didn't find a gas station on our way to the highway, which made the drive a little fraught, especially when we turned onto

Highway 97C and saw a notice that warned: Check your Fuel. Apparently there were no gas stations between there and the Okanagan Lake! We had a quarter of a tank, so we weren't too concerned until we discovered that the first half of the distance was a slow, growling climb up and up and up, consuming rather a lot of fuel, and we watched with some concern as the fuel gauge needle dipped lower and lower until we finally crested the summit at Pennask. Fortunately, it was all downhill from there, until we arrived in Kelowna. We stopped at the first gas station we could find in West Bank and filled up our very thirsty vehicle. We were laughing at ourselves; throughout our time in the north we never let the gas gauge go much under the half before filling up. How embarrassing it would have been to run out of gas when it was easily available!

We arrived at Gwen's place in Kelowna to a tumultuous welcome, and spent the whole time catching up with the news and generally chilling out and doing chores. Once we settled in, I dared to try on my dress shoes for the upcoming family wedding, but I still couldn't get them on over my injured foot (injured away back in Saskatchewan), which meant I had to go shoe shopping. What a terrible chore! I was able to find suitable replacements, so I knew I wouldn't need to break out the sneakers for that special day.

We started on a lovely and very different part of our trip: three wonderful sunny days touring a large number of wineries in the Okanagan Valley, with Gwen doing the driving. Of course, this entailed lots of tasting, and the purchasing of several bottles of wine. Three days later the RV was packed and a couple of boxes of wine were safely ensconced, ready to be taken back to Ontario.

The RV also had a bit of a spruce up and oil change in Kelowna. After all, by this time we had driven it over 10,000 km since we left home, so we felt it was due for some tender loving care.

(Above) Bob and Janet examine the results of three days of wine tasting

(Left) Janet and Gwen pose in the garden

It was hard to leave Kelowna and our friend Gwen, but now it was time to start the long drive back to Ontario. We wanted to be in Walkerton to spend some time with the family before the wedding on August 25th. However, we wanted to revisit the Icefields Parkway before we started that long trek back home. We had been through the area in 1986 with our young family, and we were interested in seeing any changes that may have occurred. We went north on Highway 97 towards Kamloops, eventually joining the Yellowhead Highway east towards Jasper.

Scenically, this was the reverse of our drive to Kelowna; we went from desert-like conditions to cooler and more forested areas, a transition that seemed to happen quite suddenly. As it became cooler, we met rain for the first time in several days. The scenery was much more mountainous, with lakes and many rivers flowing rapidly through it. A railroad ran along the valley, and we kept pace for a while with a train, with lots of empty cars and three engines, going to who knew where. After a long day of driving we finally arrived in Jasper and found a site at Whistlers, a beautiful campground, well treed and laid out. We went for a walk in the evening and reminisced about our previous visit to this area in 1986 when we were there with our three oldest children.

The next day we drove down the Icefields Parkway towards Banff, always looking unsuccessfully for wild animals. This was very different from our previous experience when it seemed that every stop meant we saw abundant wildlife.

Mountain Sheep were abundant when this photo was taken in 1986

The Athabasca Falls

On the way down the Parkway we noticed a sign for the Athabasca Falls, which merited a visit. The falls are impressive and the river is fast and furious. As we read the interpretive panels we learned that ultimately, through a somewhat tortuous route, the Athabasca joins the Peace River to form the Slave River and empties into Great Slave Lake, which drains into the Mackenzie and finally into the Beaufort Sea. This made us realize that we had seen the ultimate destination of the river so many weeks ago in Inuvik. It was hard to believe, knowing how far we had traveled, that this young river was making its way there. We remembered crossing the Athabasca in Alberta, near Whitecourt, which meant we had seen the river in the middle stage of its journey as well. Now all we needed was to see the glacier that spawned the river.

We also paused at the Sunwapta Falls, another fast flowing river creating its own canyon. As we watched the force of these rivers we understood how their power can change the landscape; carving out rocks and canyons just by the sheer volume of their waters.

The Sunwapta Falls pouring through the gorge

Gradually, with many pauses to admire spectacular views, we made our way down to the edge of the Columbia Icefield, where the Athabasca Glacier flows out. This was where our children had played in 1986! We parked the RV and walked towards the glacier, appreciating that this was the source of the Athabasca River. As we reflected on the distances we had traveled and the places we had seen, we visualized the river as a symbol of our own journey through this amazing land.

Walking and sliding on the Athabasca Glacier in 1986

As we approached the foot of the glacier we saw how much had changed over 26 years. In 1986 there were far fewer people around and virtually no commercialism. We were able to walk right up to the glacier, and watch the kids playing on it while we took pictures. Now there is a clearly delineated path with many warnings of the dangers of walking out onto the ice. Oops, maybe those signs should have been in place when we were there before! We were able to see how far the Athabasca had receded since our last visit; the place where the children had played in

1986 is now a large moraine. One sign indicated the edge of the glacier in 1992, which was likely directly below where the children had played so many years ago. Is this an indicator of climate change, or is it just part of the natural life cycle of glaciers? Either way, it is predicted that the Colombia Icefield will be gone in 100 years.

The source of the Athabaska River at the leading edge of the glacier

The Icefields Parkway is a spectacular route to drive. There are countless beautiful vistas, and at every turn in the road there is something new to see. We drove though valleys surrounded by tall, snow-capped peaks, followed rushing streams, and came upon lakes of the most astonishing colour. When you see a pure turquoise lake it looks too bright and colourful to be real, and when later you look at the photographs, you wonder if it could really have been like that.

A mountain vista along the Icefields Parkway

The colour of the lakes is hard to believe

We continued driving down towards Banff and our overnight stop, with a brief side trip to revisit Lake Louise. Everything that can be said about Lake Louise has already been said and its beauty attracts visitors from around the world. When were there in 1986 it was quite beautiful and we wanted to see it again, but this was a disappointing visit. Back in 1986 it was a quick side trip to see the lake, with no fuss or crowds. In 2012 it was difficult to even find a spot in the huge parking lot near the lake! And the walk to the water's edge reminded me of the crush of people at post-Christmas sales. All it needed was a hot dog stand, cotton candy and ice cream and it could have been any fairground anywhere.

Lake Louise failed to meet expectations. Even on a clear, sunny day the colour was not as we remembered it. False memories, or has the nature of the lake changed with its popularity?

Once we got to the lake and were able to see through the crowds of people, it simply didn't have the great colour we remembered, and had already seen earlier that day in other lakes on our drive down the Parkway. We were very disappointed; perhaps our expectations were too high, perhaps in a quieter time of the year we would have seen the lake as we remembered it?

We left Lake Louise after a very short stay and drove in the direction of Banff to find our campsite for the night on Tunnel Mountain Road. We made a brief stop at the Banff Park Museum, where we were hoping to learn more about the history of family member who was living somewhere in this area over a hundred years ago.

August 16th

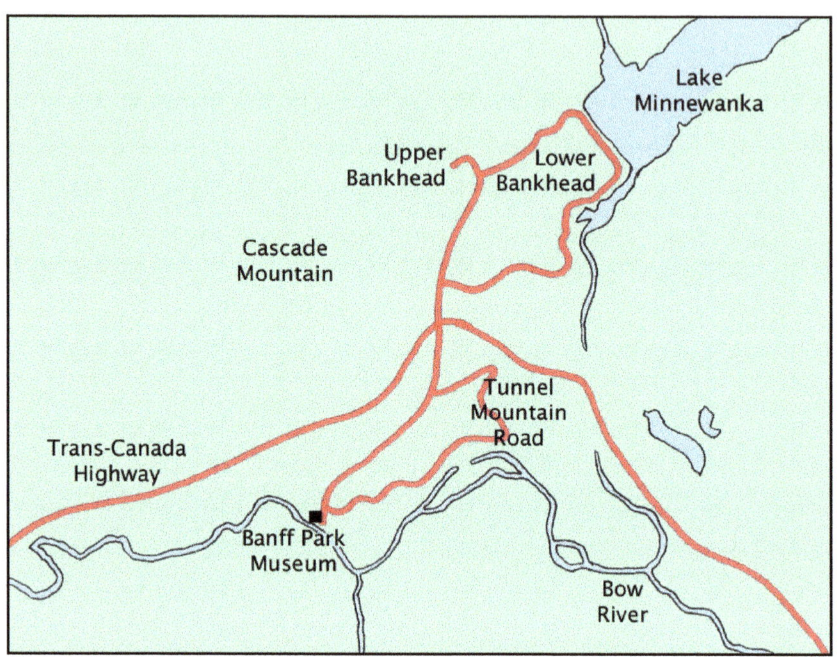

Banff/Bankhead Circuit	28km
TOTAL	28km

Chapter Fifteen
Banff and Bankhead

Following the disappointment of Lake Louise came one of the more exciting parts of our trip. My great-uncle Lewis Howells had immigrated to Canada from Wales in 1904, had lived near Banff and worked in a coal mine in the area. During his time there he had sent postcards to his sister, my grandmother Mary Howells, which depicted various aspects of his life, including scenes of the area and the mine installations. I had scanned these postcards and had the images on my laptop. I wanted to talk to the Banff Park Museum National Site of Canada staff and see if they had any knowledge of the area where Lewis had lived and worked.

Great-uncle Lewis Howells who had worked in Bankhead

We arrived at the museum late in the day and spoke to Chantal Fortier, one of the curatorial staff. I showed her some of the pictures and she recognized the areas, and pinpointed the locations on the present-day map of Banff. After a brief discussion we made an appointment to meet her the next day and spend some time going through all the pictures, learning as much as we could about my great-uncle Lewis' time in this area. We also promised to copy the pictures for her so the museum could add them to its collection.

The Banff Park Museum

Early next day we went to the museum and had time to look around and study some interesting exhibits. The theme of the museum is almost totally natural history, with stuffed animals dominating and geological specimens in smaller display cases. The historic aspects of Banff and locality are largely represented by a display of contemporary photographs and other artworks. This museum was built in 1903 and the exhibits, the interior decoration and the style have been preserved or restored to a close resemblance of the original. In 1985 it was declared a National Historic Site, and in 1986 it was classified by the Federal Heritage Buildings and Review Office in order to preserve and protect the museum for future generations. One of the exciting things we noticed on one wall was a photo of Lake Minnewanka taken at around the same time as one of the postcards from Lewis, and from more-or-less the same location!

A postcard of Lake Minnewanka (left). On the back, Lewis has written: "This is what it looks like from the Bankhead end."

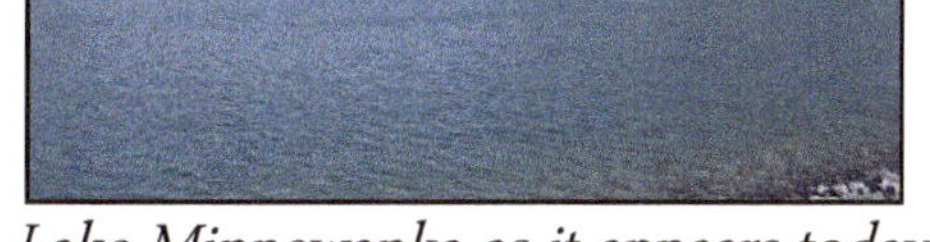

Lake Minnewanka as it appears today

We saw a sketch of the Banff Zoo from the same period showing the enclosure where a mountain lion or cougar had been housed, making Lewis's postcard on the same subject much more real.

Written on the front of the card: "Female mountain lion made her escape in 1906, [signed] Loo."

We gave Ms Fortier a memory key with scans of the postcards on it. She took time to go through the pictures with us and explain where everything was and how to get there. She found a book in the museum collection, *Bankhead: The Twenty Year Town*, and as we looked through it we recognized some of the pictures from our photographs. Suddenly I started to see what my great-uncle's life was like, and he became much more of a person and not just a signature on some old postcards.

Bankhead was a mining town. Coal was needed by the Canadian Pacific Railroad to fuel its locomotives, and a seam was found in the Cascade Mountains near Banff and Lake Minnewanka. The Canadian Pacific formed a subsidiary company, the Pacific Coal Company Ltd, and opened up a mine in this area. It was registered in 1903 and opened shortly after that. Lewis, and perhaps some of his friends from South Wales, arrived in New York in April 1903 and by 1904 he was sending postcards from Alberta to his sister in Wales.

Lewis' postcard of Gwalia House where the Welsh miners stayed

Lewis and his friends were from an area in Wales with a long history of coal mining, so it made sense that he was employed in some capacity in the mine in 1904. At this time the town of Bankhead and the mine were under construction. On one of the postcards from Lewis there is a picture of Gwalia House, so called because the men from Wales all lived there. Now I could imagine where he lived and worked.

Written on the back: "Upper town as seen from the back of this house. Lake Minnewanka in the distance." Unfortunately we don't know which house. Perhaps Gwalia?

Ms Fortier showed us how to get to the ruins of Bankhead, and to find the trail going up the mountain to an area called Upper Bankhead. The trail passes some of the old mine openings. Lower Bankhead, down in a valley, is where the foundations of some of the buildings of the industrial complex can be found. Armed with all this unexpected information we were ready to leave. However, just before we left we asked Ms Fortier where we could find a copy of *Bankhead: The Twenty Year Town*, and she very kindly gave us the copy we were holding, since it is out of print and difficult to locate now. The museum had one in better condition, which it kept for reference. This was an act of great kindness and helped me learn more about my great uncle who was a somewhat mythical figure to me.

Now we went in search of Upper Bankhead and the mine. After a short drive out of Banff we arrived at the parking lot for the facility. We started up the trail, which was nicely graveled and relatively smooth, but as we walked further up the hill the gravel on the path gave way to coal slag. At this point we knew we must be close to the mine.

The first building we came across was a concrete box, roofless and covered in graffiti, but obviously part of the mine facilities *(right)*. Later we learned this was a lantern house where miner's helmets and lamps had been stored. After each shift they were counted and if a helmet was missing it meant a miner was missing, and a search would be undertaken. It was a crude but effective way of keeping track.

Further up the hill we came across large coal tips, and soon we found one of the mine openings, likely a ventilation shaft, which had been fenced off for safety reasons. We found a second opening a little way off, also fenced. We later learned that the openings to the mines had been collapsed when the mines were closed, so we were lucky just to see as much as we did.

A ventilation shaft

Further on we came across a huge slab of concrete with lots of rusted bolts set into it, probably the base for some of the winching equipment. Some old air ducts could be seen lying around, and walking onto the coal tip revealed some ancient wooden pit props. The coal tip spread a long way, and at its furthest end we looked over the trees to see Lake Minnewanka in the distance with its distinctive mountain face coming down into the lake.

After this we went down to Lower Bankhead, the industrial side of the town. An interpretive panel described the town, and we discovered that many of the houses on site had been moved, and some relocated to Banff.

A concrete slab partially hidden by undergrowth and a section of ducting

A coal tip extending into the forest (left) at the end of which we came across the view below

There wasn't time to locate the houses that had been moved to Banff, so next time we are in this region we must check them out. We walked down the hillside to the remains of the old industrial area. It was here we learned that the coal mined from this site was full of coal tar, nasty sticky stuff and carcinogenic. The pathway around the ruins was covered in chips of coal, so it was easy to see the sticky bits! All that is left of the industrial buildings are the concrete foundations; the wooden upper structures have long since gone. We tried to guess which buildings had been used for what activity, but that was no easy task.

(Above) Concrete foundations and the remains of walls

(Left) Bankhead: The Twenty Year Town *by Ben Gadd. This book was produced by the Canadian Parks Service in association with the Coal Association of Canada. A mine of information (pun intended) of the social and industrial aspects of the town*

"Air compressor, Bankhead Power House, Pacific Coal Co. That big white patch is light from the window."

There was a mine train on display with its compressed-air locomotive and coal cars. While we knew this one was not the one Lewis worked with, it was very similar to the picture we had from all those years ago.

A detail from a postcard (left). Written on the side: "One of the motors at the mouth of the tunnel. Jack Morgan sitting on the top nearest to tunnel. Lewis in the front wearing cap."

An almost identical locomotive on display in Lower Bankfield (right)

"Some of the machine unloading output. Lewis in front with legs stuck out."

"The train leaves here at 7:55 Wednesday morning." This seems to be a joke, referring to the message on the reverse of the card.

"Bankhead upper and shops. Lower cliff of the Cascade right on picture."

Friends of Lewis on Lake Minnewanka

After Bankhead we made our way to Lake Minnewanka. This beautiful lake is obviously heavily used and appreciated by tourists. Once we had parked, we wandered down to the dam across the end of the lake, which has changed significantly since my great-uncle's time, having been dammed twice with a subsequent increase in size.

According to a plaque beside the lake, there are buildings below the water from the time when this area was so active and the town still alive. One of the postcards we have is a view of the rock coming down to the lake, and a jetty going out into the water. If it still exists, the jetty is now in the middle of the lake, but the rocks and mountains haven't changed at all, so we could imagine my great-uncle being there and seeing the mountains as we were seeing them.

Even at that time Banff was well known for its hot springs, and we have a postcard sent by Lewis showing the site when he was living in the area, although we don't know when he actually visited the springs.

Written on the back: "Hot water basin, Banff Springs:" Chantal Fortier of the Banff Park Museum identified the caretaker, standing in the rear, as David Drummond Gallatly

It is fascinating to think that the town of Bankfield was an active mining town for only 20 years. The mine closed in 1922 following a strike by the workers. There was a slump in the industry, the Canadian Pacific Railroad had located better coal elsewhere, and the mine at Bankfield was expensive to run. It had become less economical to produce coal, so the strike seemed to act as the catalyst for the mine's closing. By this time my uncle had long since moved from Bankhead. I discovered census records from 1911 that placed both him and his wife in North Battleford, Saskatchewan.

Having explored the upper levels of the mine and the ruins of the industrial structures below, we returned slowly to the parking lot, talking and thinking about what we had seen. This was really exciting; I had never met my great-uncle Lewis, but to see where his postcards had come from in 1904/5 was really amazing. I had never dreamed of actually seeing this, and I would have loved to have shared it with both my late grandmother and mother. They, too, would have appreciated knowing where Lewis had worked and lived!

This was the last major excitement of the trip. We were beginning to feel the pressure of getting to the wedding on time, so after seeing Bankhead we started traveling east to get ourselves back to Ontario with enough time to make ourselves presentable. After a long afternoon's driving, we found a campsite near the Royal Tyrrell Museum in Drumheller, which we had planned to visit on our way home.

August 16th to August 22nd

Banff to Drumheller	267km
Drumheller to Swift Current	543km
Swift Current to Portage la Prairie	740km
Portage la Prairie to Kakabeka Falls	751km
Kakabeka Falls to Wawa	498km
Wawa to Tobermory	582km
Tobermory to Owen Sound	136km
TOTAL	3,517km

Chapter Sixteen
Banff to Owen Sound

After our exciting day of discovery in Banff, we were off to the Royal Tyrrell Museum, famous for its dinosaur collection. As we drove into the Badlands we found the landscape quite different from any other we had seen. The sandstone in this region has been sculpted by time into fantastic shapes called hoodoos, which expose the layering of the rock as parts of it have been eroded. The museum lies right in the middle of this wonderfully weird landscape and fits right into the environment.

The Royal Tyrrell Museum fits into its environment

On entering the building the visitors follow a 'path' through the collections and see the fossils laid out in chronological order. The labeling is very informative and the variety and number of dinosaurs is staggering. We were totally impressed and very glad we took the time to visit the collection here.

One of the beautifully laid out dinosaur skeletons

We decided to have lunch at the museum before continuing eastwards. A little gopher chose to entertain all the diners by begging for his lunch. He ran up to one lady who gave him a chip, but instead of letting go of the chip she held on to it.

The gopher was not amused and put his little paws up and pushed her away! The chip broke and he ran off with his piece to wherever his nest was. We were all laughing at his antics, and the lady made a comment on the softness of his fur and paws. It made me wish the gopher had come to my table instead.

At one level we were looking forward to getting back home and enjoying the wedding on the way, but another part of us wanted further exploration of this wonderful country. As we drove and relished the great open spaces, we suddenly understood this openness was something we had missed; the mountains we had been driving through for the last few weeks were spectacular, and we had loved our time in them, but now we really enjoyed the peace of the flat landscape and the calmness and order of the farmlands. We were in the prairies of the mid-west where the horizon goes on forever, and we were reveling in the flat roads and easy driving. All we had to do was put the RV in cruise and just point it in the general direction of Ontario.

Our first overnight stop was in Swift Current, where we saw a wonderful sunset and some interesting old farming equipment rusting away in the campground.

A beautiful sunset over Swift Current, rather evocative of the last stages of our trip

Then it was on to Portage la Prairie for the night, and a relaxing swim in the campground pool. The next day, as we drove through Winnipeg, we were amused to come across some really bad roads; so bad that our cupboard doors were shaken open again, something we hadn't experienced since Alaska. The road surface improved as we left Winnipeg, heading to our next overnight stop in Kakabeka Falls, Ontario.

Kakabeka Falls was our last chance for a trip down memory lane. In that marvelous, never-to-be-forgotten journey across Canada in 1986, we had camped there. It was a very cold night on that occasion, probably about 5°C, and we had built the biggest campfire ever, or at least the children thought so at the time! So, after settling in to the campsite, we walked to the waterfalls and then to the museum, thinking about that last visit when our youngest daughter, Heather, was accidentally locked in the building. Fortunately she was rescued quite rapidly, but even today she remembers that experience.

Kakabeka Falls

After an evening of reminiscing, we left Kakabeka Falls and continued east. Our initial plan was to stop somewhere between Wawa and Manitoulin Island for the night. However, there was a delay. Just outside Nipigon we joined a huge traffic jam and it was clear that nobody was going anywhere for quite some time; everything was stopped in both directions and the gossip mill was in full swing. We later learned that someone had stolen fuel from a gas station in Wawa, 200-300km up the road, and the police had shut the highway down and laid spike blankets in the road to stop him. After about an hour the police allowed traffic through and we were on our way, although we wondered what the real reason was for all that fuss. It couldn't just have just been over some stolen gas.

As we left Nipigon we passed a car impaled on a guardrail and, being in the habit of stopping, we checked it out. Fortunately there no one was in the car and someone had placed a pylon in the road to warn other traffic. Another driver stopped to make sure we were fine. He had recognized our RV from the Nipigon line up, and was concerned. Stopping to check out stranded motorists had become a habit during our driving through the North, and we appreciated his concern.

We decided to stop for the night in Wawa (of giant goose statue fame) and take the next couple of days to get to Owen Sound. We left the next morning, planning to stay overnight on Manitoulin Island and cross over by ferry to Tobermory on the Bruce Peninsula the following day. However, as we drove through Manitoulin we realized we might have a chance to catch the ferry to Tobermory that evening. A few minutes after finding the ferry terminal we were in the line-up for our 11th and final ferry trip of the vacation. To amuse ourselves we read all the tourist information on the ferry and found advertisements for glass-bottom boat trips to the Flower Pots and sunken wrecks, so this would be our final excursion before meeting the family. Once off the ferry we made the necessary booking, found our campsite and had a long talk on the phone with the family regarding pre- and post-wedding plans.

Our 11th and final ferry, a short trip to Tobermory

The trip on the glass bottom boat was the icing on the cake. It was totally unanticipated and a lot of fun. It started with floating over a couple of sunken ships in the harbour. They were in fairly shallow water, which made them easier to see from above. The deck and hold of the first wreck were easily seen by just looking into the water, but through the glass-bottom of the boat much more detail, especially the planking of the ship's deck, could be clearly seen. We passed over a couple more ships in the harbour, and then headed for Flowerpot Island.

The glass-bottomed boat and a view of the timbers of a shallow shipwreck

The Flowerpots are rock formations that have been worn away by the water and, as the name suggests, resemble extremely large flowerpots. As the boat was heading towards them the guide spoke about the history of the area and indicated points of interest. He outlined the history of the lighthouses, and told us that the last manned lighthouse in the area was closed down in the 1990s. Some older lighthouses have been replaced with more the modern automated versions; these are very basic structures of metal painted red and white. While they don't look like 'real' lighthouses, they are very efficient and do the job well.

Automated lighthouses just don't cut it for scenic or nostalgic value

Up close the flowerpots look as if they are made of blocks of stone piled on one another. These formations are somewhat reminiscent of the Hopewell Cape rocks in the Bay of Fundy in New Brunswick, but are much craggier. The Hopewell Cape formations are softer looking due to the constant action of the tides.

A prominent flower pot at the end of the island from two angles

We went right around the island and then returned to Tobermory. Again, the commentary from the guides kept us entertained while we watched the scenery go by. Apparently the homes on the edge of the water are permanent and not the usual summer cottages one would expect, which was a surprise; lovely in the summer, but likely not as nice in the winter with the winds coming from the north. Back at the dock we made a quick side trip the museum/information centre of the National Park, and spent a happy hour examining all the exhibits. Attached to the museum was a tall fire watchtower, open to the public, so Bob climbed up to the top and enjoyed the panoramic view of the tip of the Bruce Peninsula.

The view from the top of the watchtower

We had lunch and set out towards Owen Sound and Bob's family. We spent a lovely evening catching up with the family and being updated on all the plans for the coming celebrations.

August 22nd to August 27th

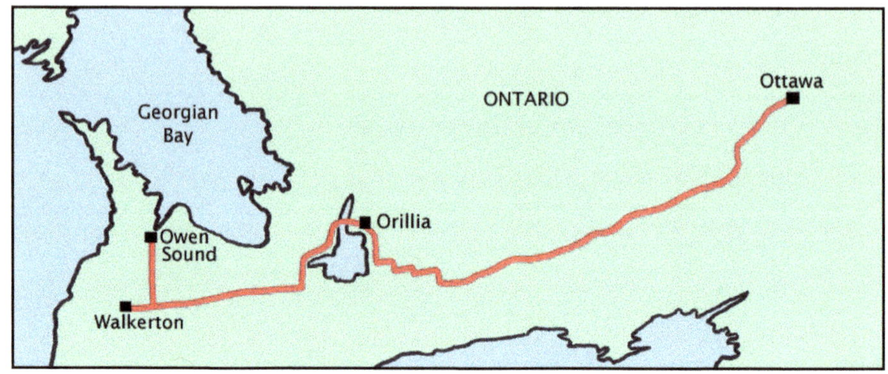

Owen Sound to Walkerton	119km
Walkerton to Orillia	176km
Orillia to Ottawa	390km
TOTAL	685km

Chapter Seventeen
Owen Sound to Home

In the morning we spent some time in Owen Sound with the family and were shown around the gaming store, Scenic City Games, (*below*) owned and operated by Bob's nephew, Geoff.

The millrace and waterfall at Inglis Falls (below)

We left Owen Sound later in the morning and drove to Walkerton, stopping for a picnic lunch at Inglis Falls. This is an attractive historic site with a preserved mill from the 19th century, and we enjoyed walking around and learning some of the industrial history of this area. Once we arrived in Walkerton it was time to get ourselves organized for the wedding. Before we started this long journey we realized we would need time to make ourselves presentable. Reservations were made at Best Western and time allowed for essential tasks: haircuts, pedicures, manicures, etc. So appointments were made. After all, we were representing our side of the family.

The following morning we started on this task (as best we could, given our seniority). While returning to our vehicle, a lady on the street recognized us as visitors to Walkerton—not surprising 'since we were driving an RV—and spoke highly of a winery to the south of the town which we 'absolutely must visit'. We followed her good suggestion and regaled ourselves with a whole selection of beverages to taste; ciders and fruit wines, as well the traditional wine made from grapes. It was a fun experience, and while we were surprised to find a winery in this area, it made sense as the grape-growing ecosystem of the Niagara Escarpment actually extends this far north.

While walking around Walkerton we came across some very fine murals depicting historical scenes from the town's history

It was now August 25, 2012, our niece Kimberley's wedding day. We were up early and went down for breakfast in the hotel dining room, where we met a number of wedding guests who were also in town for the big day. After a quiet morning it was time to get ready for the ceremony.

While we got cleaned and dressed up for the great occasion, we were laughing at ourselves because we figured that we and our clothes had traveled over 16,000 km just for this occasion! It was somewhat ironic, since normally it would only take us about seven to eight hours to cover just over 600 km from home.

The father of the bride leads his daughter down the aisle. The happy couple during the ceremony

The church service was lovely; Kimberley's husband-to-be, Chad, was the pastor of this church so many of his parishioners were there to see him get married. The service was beautiful and the organist played some very fine music. As always the bride was radiant, and the groom very serious. After the service and the requisite photography session it was time for the reception in a local hall. This was a lot of fun and I was able to keep my promise to Kimberley that I would dance at the wedding. I did, damaged foot and all. Bob and I maintained the family tradition of being the first on the dance floor and the last off! Finally, it was time to go. The big day was over, and now Kim and Chad were about to start on their new journey.

Surprisingly, we were up early the next day. It was time to head home, but before we started the drive back to Ottawa we spent a happy few hours with the family at the wedding present opening. Many of Chad's parishioners acknowledged this special time for him with cards and small gifts; it was really touching. After many farewells we headed off to Orillia for our final night on the road. We reminisced about this amazing journey, and kept wondering what had been the 'best thing' about the trip. After around 20 'best things' we just laughed and decided the whole trip was the Best Thing. We stopped just outside Orillia at our last overnight campground.

The last night in the RV

Our final day of driving was shorter than most but felt longer, no doubt because we knew the 'real' world would once again be with us, bringing a complete change from the last several weeks. Finally, the RV was parked in the driveway at home and we sat down with a cup of tea and a huge pile of mail! We were home after eight weeks and three days of traveling!

As we reviewed our journey we checked our travel statistics: We had driven nearly 17,000km; visited five states in the US and five provinces and two territories in Canada; crossed the Canada/US border eight times; taken 11 ferries and crossed 15 major rivers; and had seen two oceans, the Pacific and the Arctic. We had met many fascinating and interesting people on the way, and found kindness and goodwill everywhere we went. We saw places we had only dreamed about, others we knew from earlier times, and yet more that forged links with family history. It was a true voyage of discovery.

Even though we had been away just over eight weeks, it felt as if a lifetime of experiences had occurred since our departure. When we left Ottawa summer had just started, and now the nights were becoming cooler and the days, although warm, were definitely showing signs of cooling down as well. The trees were starting to change their colours, the grasses had gone that golden colour of late summer, and we realized in our absence the seasons really had changed. While all this was happening, we had been in the land of the midnight sun; we had seen glaciers, mountains, and many varied landscapes from the tundra to the prairies to the mountains. We had seen ways of life so very different from the life we live in Ottawa, and we had come to understand how important diverse modes of transport are in the far flung areas of the continent. It has been a never-to-be-forgotten journey of living in and understanding the many regions of this huge country.

Resources

Ben Gadd (1989) *BANKHEAD The Twenty Year Town*, The Coal Association of Canada, Calgary, Alberta, in cooperation with Canadian Parks Service, Banff National Park, Alberta. ISBN: 0-969-0845-5-2

Michael Gates (2012), *Dalton's Gold Rush Trail*, Madeira Park, BC: Harbour Publishing. ISBN: 978-1-55017-570-7

Michael Gates (2010), *History Hunting in the Yukon*, Madeira Park, BC: Harbour Publishing. ISBN: 978-1-55017-477-9

Hazel Johnson (2009) *RV-ing and Other Adventures North of 60,* Ottawa: Baico Publishing. ISBN: 978-1-926596-10-5

Kris Valencia (ed) (2012),*The Milepost* , Augusta, GA: William S. Morris III.

A Note on the Lost Patrol

On December 21st 1910 Inspector Frank Fitzgerald of the Royal Canadian Mounted Police, an experienced northern traveler, together with Richard Taylor, George Kinney and ex-Mountie Sam Carter as guide, set off from Fort McPherson with three dog teams for Dawson City, Yukon. Unable to find the right pass through the mountains, the patrol ran short of supplies and eventually turned back, but too late. They all perished and are buried below a memorial in the Anglican church of Fort McPherson, Northwest Territories.

The song *Fly Like an Eagle* by Chris Philpotts evokes their fate:

My name is Richard Taylor and the story is told
How I left Fort McPherson on the Dawson Patrol.
Our leader was Fitzgerald, no finer Mountie in the land
Mushing thirty days to Dawson with dispatches in our hand.
But when those days were over, we still fought the bitter cold
I wish that I'd had wings to leave the Lost Patrol.
A good trip on the train you average twenty miles a day
But bad weather came and went and overflow caused delay.
Our guide Samuel Carter missed the cut-off for the Peel!
So we hired Esau George to come and take us there for real.
We were nine days behind schedule, with each day we were losing ground
I wish that I'd had wings so I could turn around.

And I'd fly, fly, fly like an eagle
Up the mighty Peel River to the warmth of my home
And rest myself in the glow of the fire

And never more would I roam.
Six days we searched for Forest Creek along the Little Wind
But Carter couldn't find it so we turned around again
Why Fitzgerald trusted Carter I'll never understand
For he sealed our fate forever, made us legends in this land.
We headed back for McPherson, killing dogs to keep us fed
I wish that I had wings so I could fly instead.
At sixty-five below a man's breath will freeze his face
The cold will cut right through, it will snap a snowshoe lace
The mist will make him blind, his progress becomes slow
Disaster lies awaiting in the cruel northern snow
They sent Dempster out from Dawson to find the Lost Patrol
Twenty miles past Colin's cabin, he found a kerchief in the snow
And when they came upon our camp, my face they could not see
For I'd saved myself from starving with a shot... from a 303
One body lay there with me and two more up the trail
I wish that I'd had wings and never told this tale.
And I'd fly, fly, fly like an eagle
Up the mighty Peel River to the warmth of my home
And rest myself in the glow of the fire
And never more would I roam.

Northern Tracks, The Gumboots, CD: GBTD 7002

www.ingramcontent.com/pod-product-compliance
Ingram Content Group UK Ltd.
Pitfield, Milton Keynes, MK11 3LW, UK
UKHW062303290726
14090UKWH00017B/868